Oliver Cromwell.

Classics of Reformed Spirituality

"To honour God"
The spirituality of Oliver Cromwell
Michael A.G. Haykin

Forthcoming

The letters of George Whitefield
Selections from the sermons of Alexander Whyte
The hymns of Ann Griffiths

Michael A.G. Haykin, series editor

Classics of Reformed Spirituality

"To honour God"

The spirituality of Oliver Cromwell

Edited and introduced by

Michael A.G. Haykin

Dundas, Ontario

Joshua Press Inc., Dundas, Ontario

Published 1999
Printed in Canada

Editorial director: Michael A.G. Haykin
Creative/production manager: Janice Van Eck

Frontispiece is a portion of the Cromwell Window at Emmanuel United Reformed Church, Cambridge, England.

Canadian Cataloguing in Publication Data

Cromwell, Oliver, 1599–1658
"To honour God": the spirituality of Oliver Cromwell

(Classics of Reformed spirituality)
Includes bibliographical references and index.
ISBN 1-894400-03-8

1. Cromwell, Oliver, 1599–1658 — Contributions to spirituality. 2. Spirituality. I. Haykin, Michael A.G. II. Title. III. Series

BX9339.C76A25 1999 248'.092 C99–931407–6

In memory of William E. Payne (1938–1997),
godly pastor, Spirit-anointed preacher and dear friend,
who would have loved to have written the foreword
for a book on his hero, Oliver, but who now has something
far better, "the happiness we all pant after."

Contents

In the midst of all the changes and mutations which the infinitely wise providence of God doth daily effect in the greater and lesser things of this world, as to the communication of his love in Jesus Christ, and the merciful, gracious distributions of the unsearchable riches of grace, and the hid treasures thereof purchased by his blood, he knows no repentance. Of both these you have had full experience; and though your concernment in the former hath been as eminent as that of any person whatever in these later ages of the world, yet your interest in and acquaintance with the latter is, as of incomparable more importance in itself, so answerably of more value and esteem unto you.

John Owen to Oliver Cromwell, 1654

Oliver Cromwell

An engraving based on the Samuel Cooper miniature. [Reproduced from the frontispiece of Thomas Carlyle, *Oliver Cromwell's Letters and Speeches with Elucidations* (New York: Charles Scribner's Sons, 1897), I]

Preface
"Warts and everything"

When Samuel Cooper (1609–1672), the great miniaturist, was painting his famous portrait of Oliver Cromwell (1599–1658), the Puritan leader is reported to have said, "I desire you would use all your skill to paint my picture truly like me and flatter me not at all. But [pointing to his own face] remark all these roughness, pimples, warts and everything as you see me. Otherwise I will never pay a farthing for it."[1] The story may well be apocryphal, but it has an authentic Cromwellian ring to it. Just as Cromwell admonished the artist to paint a true likeness of his outward appearance, so he would urge anyone studying his inner life to view it "warts and everything."

There is, for instance, no doubt that Cromwell's Calvinist convictions were central to his life, both public and private,[2] and that he knew himself to be among God's saints. He would have readily agreed with his Puritan contemporary, the Welsh preacher Walter Cradock (*c.*1610–1659), who once stated: "The greatest difference…in all the Book of God, between Saints and Sinners is, that the one hath the Spirit, and the other hath not."[3] And Cromwell knew on which side of the divide he had been placed. And yet, he was always vividly aware of his own unworthiness, his own shortcomings, and his failings. "The best of us," he once remarked to Philip Wharton (1613–1690), are "poor, weak saints."[4] He did not hesitate to describe himself as a "poor worm and weak servant,"[5] one who was characterized by "weaknesses,...inordinate passions," and "unskilfulness and everyway unfitness" for his calling.[6] And on his deathbed he could confess, "I think I am the poorest wretch that lives."[7]

This selection of texts relating to Cromwell's spirituality thus has no intention of being hagiographical. That would be both false to the facts and a betrayal of the intent expressed in Cromwell's confessional remarks cited above, namely his desire to live a life of Christian integrity. On the other hand, it does seek to recommend certain aspects of Cromwell's spirituality as a model for believers today, for the author is convinced that his spiritual vision, and that of the Puritans in general, still possesses ongoing value for the contemporary church.

Spirituality lay at the very core of English Puritanism.[8] Whatever else the Puritans may have been—social, political, and ecclesiastical Reformers—they were primarily men and women intensely passionate about piety and Christian experience. And as will be seen in the extracts from Cromwell's writings, he is no exception. He is quintessentially Puritan.

The edition from which the selections from Cromwell's written corpus have been taken is that of

Thomas Carlyle, *Oliver Cromwell's Letters and Speeches with Elucidations* (New York: Charles Scribner's Sons, 1897), 4 volumes. A more recent edition of Cromwell's letters and speeches, that of Wilbur Cortez Abbott with Catherine D. Crane and Madeleine R. Gleason, *The Writings and Speeches of Oliver Cromwell* (Cambridge: Harvard University Press, 1937–1947), 4 volumes, has been employed to make minor corrections in the text of the Carlyle edition.[9] Other changes to the Carlyle edition have been solely in terms of modernising the punctuation and capitalization. Obsolete or archaic words have been retained and their meanings given in explanatory footnotes. In addition, two of the selections below have been drawn from the Abbott edition. For permission to use these texts, I am grateful to Harvard University Press, Cambridge, Massachusetts.

The background on the front and back covers is a contemporary drawing executed by Deborah Livingston-Lowe of Toronto. It is based on a seventeenth-century pattern of English embroidery. The frontispiece is a photograph of the Cromwell Window in Emmanuel United Reformed Church, Cambridge, England. I would like to thank the church for permission to use this photograph, Hilary Bugden for arranging to have the photograph taken and Mike Prodigalidad for taking it.

Thanks are also due Janice Van Eck in the design and layout of the book, Virginia Ho of Heritage Baptist College and Theological Seminary Library, Cambridge, Ontario, Canada, in tracking down a reference, Hetty Payne for the gift of some books relating to Cromwell, and John Goldsmith of the Cromwell Museum, Huntingdon, Cambridgeshire, England, for information.

[1] Antonia Fraser, *Cromwell. Our Chief of Men* (London: Weidenfeld and Nicolson, 1973), 472.
[2] Roger Howell, Jr., "Cromwell's Personality: The Problems and Promises of a Psychohistorical Approach" in R.C. Richardson, ed., *Images of Oliver Cromwell. Essays for and by Roger Howell, Jr.* (Manchester/New York: Manchester University Press, 1993), 139.
[3] Geoffrey F. Nuttall, *The Holy Spirit in Puritan Faith and Experience* (2nd ed.; Oxford: Basil Blackwell, 1947), 142.
[4] See p.67.
[5] See p.79.
[6] See p.90.
[7] See p.126. See also B.A. Ramsbottom, "Oliver Cromwell—The Man, His Character and Beliefs," *The Evangelical Quarterly*, 27 (1955), 31.
[8] Irvonwy Morgan, *Puritan Spirituality* (London: Epworth Press, 1973), 53–65; Dewey D. Wallace, Jr., *The Spirituality of the Later English Puritans. An Anthology* (Macon, Georgia: Mercer University Press, 1987), xi–xiv; J.I. Packer, *A Quest for Godliness: The Puritan Vision of the Christian Life* (Wheaton, Illinois: Crossway Books, 1990), 37–38. For other studies of their spirituality or aspects of it, see especially Nuttall, *Holy Spirit in Puritan Faith and Experience*; idem, "The Holy Spirit in Puritan Piety" in his *The Puritan Spirit. Essays and Addresses* (London: Epworth Press, 1967), 95–103; Gordon Rupp, "A Devotion of Rapture in English Puritanism" in R. Buick Knox, ed., *Reformation, Conformity and Dissent. Essays in honour of Geoffrey Nuttall* (London: Epworth Press, 1977), 115–131; Garth B. Wilson, "The Puritan Doctrine of the Holy Spirit: A Critical Investigation

of a Crucial Chapter in the History of Protestant Theology" (Unpublished Th.D. Thesis, Knox College, The Toronto School of Theology, 1978); R. Tudur Jones, "Union with Christ: The Existential Nerve of Puritan Piety," *Tyndale Bulletin*, 41 (1990), 186–208.

[9] Neither of these editions are what can be called critical editions. For the problems with both of these editions as critical editions, see John Morrill, "Textualizing and Contextualizing Cromwell," *The Historical Journal*, 33 (1990), 629–639.

"To honour God": The spirituality of Oliver Cromwell

In a recent collection of essays dealing with "counterfactual" history, John Adamson, a Cambridge University scholar who specializes in the political and cultural history of seventeenth century Britain, has an intriguing essay entitled "England without Cromwell: What if Charles I had avoided the Civil War?"[1] He reasons that if Charles I (1600–1649) had been able to avoid the Civil War, the evolution of England's constitutional monarchy, in which power came to be shared between the crown and parliament, may well have been set back decades, even centuries. And England could have ended up being a mirror image of Louis XIV's absolutist France across the Channel. Similarly, Kevin Phillips, in a significant study of the role of religious dissent in Anglo-American civil wars, notes how different history would have been if Oliver Cromwell had emigrated to New England as he actually thought of doing as late as 1641. The English Civil War would have been very different, and as a result, the American Revolution and the American Civil War might never have happened.[2] But Cromwell did not emigrate to the new world, and his Ironside cavalry did shatter the Royalist cause at the Battles of Marston Moor and Naseby and the history of the English-speaking peoples was forever changed.

Of course, Cromwell, imbued as he was with a deep sense of God's providential ordering of the world, would probably have considered such reflections frivolous. God's purposes for his life, despite what he considered his "unskilfulness and everyway unfitness,"[3] were that he eventually occupy a position critical to the spiritual state of England. Cromwell's rise to power is quite remarkable. This is especially so in view of the fact that, as John Morrill has convincingly shown, Cromwell's status in 1640 when the alarms of civil war began to sound in England was much humbler than has generally been assumed.[4] In the words of Morrill, he "spent the 1620s and 1630s in largely silent pain at his personal lot and at the drift of public affairs."[5] He had significant financial problems during this period as well as being somewhat sickly, and was living in relative obscurity. That such a man with little rank or standing would rise to the historical prominence that he later occupied is, even to the jaundiced, secular eye of much modern historiography, nothing short of amazing. To Cromwell, it was only explainable by the sovereign hand of God.

In the following reflection on Cromwell's spirituality, this providentialist reading of both private and public history is the natural place to begin, for it dominated his spiritual life. We then look at Cromwell's conversion, the place where he consciously committed himself to be a servant of this providence. As he sought to live for God in the trauma of the English Civil War, he embraced at least two goals that gave further shape to his spiritual vision that we wish to consider. First, there was his desire to promote heart-religion, a vital Christianity in which substance and the Spirit were central, not form and church structures. And then, linked to this, he sought to create an environment where there might be genuine liberty of conscience.[6]

"We follow the Lord who goeth before" *A providentialist spirituality*

A firm belief in divine providence was the bread and butter of the Puritanism of Cromwell's day. To give but one instance, the early Stuart Puritan Richard Sibbes (1577–1635) could state on the basis of Matthew 10:29–30 that God's "providence extends to the smallest things, to the sparrows and to the hair of our heads; he governs every particular passage of our lives."[7] Similarly Cromwell could urge Robert Blake (1598–1657) and Edward Montagu (1625–1672), key naval commanders in the Cromwellian government, to rely wholeheartedly on God's providential care. It will be salutary,

Cromwell writes, for them to submit all of their

> affairs to the disposition of our All-wise Father; who, not only out of prerogative, but because of his wisdom, goodness and truth, ought to be resigned unto by his creatures, and most especially by those who are children of his begetting through the Spirit. ...Indeed all the dispensations of God, whether adverse or prosperous, do fully read that lesson. We can no more turn away the Evil, as we call it, than attain the Good.[8]

Here, Cromwell is not so much discounting the place of human endeavours and abilities, as seeking to inculcate distrust in them and total reliance on God's sovereign out-working of his purposes in every moment of time. As Cromwell had written to Richard Maijor (1604–1660), the father of one of his daughters-in-law: "Truly our work is neither from our brains nor from our courage and strength, but we follow the Lord who goeth before, and gather what he scattereth."[9]

This passage from Cromwell's letter to Maijor was written in the midst of Cromwell's campaign in Ireland, undertaken in 1649 and 1650 to prevent an invasion of England by Irish troops loyal to the future Charles II (1630–1685). It reflects another key aspect of Cromwell's providentialism, namely, the conviction that often God reveals his providential will in military victory. Thus, after the Battle of

Marston Moor in 1644, Cromwell wrote to his brother-in-law, Valentine Walton (died *c.*1661) that the victory was "a great favour from the Lord." He thus could urge Walton, "Give glory, all the glory, to God." Likewise, after the other major parliamentary victory in the first phase of the Civil War, the Battle of Naseby, in June 1645, Cromwell told William Lenthall (1591–1662), the Speaker of the House of Commons: "this is none other but the hand of God; and to him alone belongs the glory."[10] In 1655 Cromwell summed up his view of these military victories and those that followed during the second phase of the Civil War from 1648 to 1651: these victories were not "human designs… These issues and events have not been forecast; but [were] sudden Providences."[11]

Cromwell's overall conviction about the sovereignty of God in all human affairs is certainly biblical and admirable. Yet, is God always on the side of the victors? Does success invariably indicate divine approval? Few Evangelical Christians today would be prepared to give an unequivocal yes to these questions.[12] It strikes this writer that a more biblical perspective is one that Cromwell expressed near the end of his life when, in the spring of 1657, it was suggested to him that he restore the monarchy in his person and become King Oliver I. After much prayer and apparent indecision, he rejected this offer. During his struggle to discern what exactly God wanted him to do, he said: "who can love to walk in the dark? But Providence doth often so dispose."[13] This statement is a clear assertion of God's sovereign involvement in every event of an individual's life and the history of a people. But it is also a recognition that those who confess this providential sovereignty are not always able to discern the exact path it is taking.

"One beam in a dark place" *A spirituality rooted in conversion*

Oliver Cromwell was born in Huntingdon, in East Anglia, on April 25, 1599, the only surviving son of a gentleman, Robert Cromwell (d.1617), who, in turn, was the younger son of a knight, Sir Henry Cromwell. Despite these gentry connections, however, Cromwell's early years were spent on the fringes of East Anglian landowners. His economic status was far more precarious than has generally been thought and his social links appear to have been with what was called the "middling sort," urban merchants and working farmers. Exemplifying these connections is his marriage to Elizabeth Bourchier (1599–1665) in 1620, the daughter of a successful London fur-dealer.[14]

As for the role of religion in his upbringing, it used to be assumed that he had received a thoroughly Puritan education at the hands of Thomas Beard (*c.*1565–1632), the local schoolmaster.[15] In fact, as John Morrill has now shown in some detail, Beard was the very antithesis of the Puritan pastor:

a covetous man who lived in a grand style, with little interest in what was important to the Puritans, namely the ongoing reformation of the Church of England.[16] Nor is there any clear indication that his parents were strongly inclined towards Puritanism.[17] What we do know with certainty is that between 1628 and 1634 Cromwell underwent an evangelical conversion that would be the dominant influence over the rest of his life.[18]

Thankfully, we are not in the dark about the impact of this conversion, for Cromwell discussed his experience in a letter to his cousin, Elizabeth St. John, in 1638:

> [T]o honour my God by declaring what he hath done for my soul, in this I am confident, and I will be so. Truly, then, this I find: That he giveth springs in a dry and barren wilderness where no water is. I live (you know where) in Mesheck, which they say signifies *Prolonging*; in Kedar, which signifies *Blackness*: yet the Lord forsaketh me not. Though he do prolong, yet he will I trust bring me to his tabernacle, to his resting-place. My soul is with the congregation of the firstborn, my body rests in hope, and if here I may honour my God either by doing or by suffering, I shall be most glad.
>
> Truly no poor creature hath more cause to put forth himself in the cause of his God than I. I have had plentiful wages beforehand, and I am sure I shall never earn the least mite. The

> Lord accept me in his Son, and give me to walk in the light,—and give us to walk in the light, as he is the light! He it is that enlighteneth our blackness, our darkness. I dare not say, he hideth his face from me. He giveth me to see light in his light. One beam in a dark place hath exceeding much refreshment in it:—blessed be his name for shining upon so dark a heart as mine! You know what my manner of life hath been. Oh, I lived in and loved darkness, and hated the light. I was a chief, the chief of sinners. This is true; I hated godliness, yet God had mercy on me. O the riches of his mercy! Praise him for me;—pray for me, that he who hath begun a good work would perfect it to the day of Christ.[19]

What is unmistakable about this Scripture-saturated text is that it records an unforgettable event.[20] We are not told how, but Cromwell came to see that at the core of his being was darkness and a love of sin. So great was this love for sin that he found Paul's words in 1 Timothy 1:15 the most apt description of his state: he was "the chief of sinners." Cromwell's use of this phrase should not be taken to imply that he led the unrestrained life of a libertine before his conversion, for which there is no evidence.[21] But nor is it mere hyperbole. In the light of God's goodness and the riches of his mercy, Cromwell can but view his pre-conversion experience as a sink of sin.

In a fine study of "Cromwell's religion," J.C. Davis

makes the assertion that "Cromwell's private religious thinking and devotion are sparsely documented."[22] This is not exactly the case, as is evident from the texts reproduced in this book. They reveal that his conversion gave him a profound understanding of God. For Cromwell, he is both a "great and glorious God," who alone is "worthy to be feared and trusted,"[23] and also a Father who is "merciful, long-suffering, abundant in goodness and truth, forgiving iniquity, transgression and sin."[24] These attributes were in full display in God's covenantal work of salvation, so utterly undeserved by sinners. The covenant that God makes with Christ for the elect is a unilateral covenant in which God "undertakes all, and the poor soul nothing."[25] The sovereignty of God in salvation thus becomes the sinner's place of rest, not only at conversion, but for the rest of his or her life. As he tells his son-in-law, Charles Fleetwood (*c.*1618–1692), in 1652:

> [S]hall we seek for the root of our comforts within us; what God hath done, what he is to us in Christ, is the root of our comfort. In this is stability; in us is weakness. Acts of obedience are not perfect, and therefore yield not perfect peace. Faith, as an act, yields it not, but as it carries us into him, who is our perfect rest and peace; in whom we are accounted of, and received by, the Father, even as Christ himself. This is our high calling. Rest we here, and here only.[26]

Three years later he can again write to Fleetwood, and tell him that his salvation consists in this one thing: that "God is bound in faithfulness to Christ, and in him to us; the covenant is without us, a transaction between God and Christ." Thus, despite daily "sins and infirmities," Cromwell, like all other believers, can "have peace and safety, and apprehension of love, from a Father in covenant, who cannot deny himself."[27]

Cromwell has various ways of describing the experience of entry into and standing fast in this covenant. In his letter to Elizabeth St. John he uses the imagery of illumination: God converting the heart by giving light and so dispelling spiritual darkness. In other texts he can talk of the light of God's countenance being better than life.[28] Alongside this imagery of light, Cromwell also uses the images of heat and flame. On one occasion when he wrote to his daughter Bridget (1624–1662) in 1646, he tells her to "press on" after Christ and "let not husband, let not anything cool thy affections." He expresses the hope that Bridget's husband, his close confidant Henry Ireton (1611–1651), will in fact be used to "inflame" them.[29]

In other texts, the imagery is drawn from the realms of sense and taste. In his 1655 letter to Charles Fleetwood, for example, he depicts the activity of the enlightened soul as "leaning upon the Son, or looking to him, thirsting after him, embracing him."[30] He is convinced that those who have "tasted that the Lord is gracious" will be "pressing [on] after [the] full enjoyment" of him.[31] Finally, in one of the most moving expressions of his faith, Cromwell sums up what conversion means for the believer. It gives him or her a life-long passion to enjoy God in heaven. Writing to his brother-in-law, Valentine Walton, to inform him of the death of his son during the Battle of Marston Moor, he tells him that the Lord has taken his son "into the happiness we all pant after and live for."[32]

"To honour my God either by doing or suffering" *A spirituality of activism*

What is also noteworthy about Cromwell's testimony of conversion in his letter to his cousin is that he states that the new birth gave him a desire to live henceforth for God, or in his words, "to honour my God either by doing or suffering." The Civil War and its aftermath, which saw Cromwell's appointment as Lord Protector, provided the Puritan leader with ample opportunities for this. Two particular areas that relate to spirituality deserve mention.

First, there was what J.C. Davis has termed Cromwell's "antiformalism," his conviction that a "Christianity of substance, of the heart and spirit" is what should occupy the major efforts and activities of God's children.[33] One of the first texts that enunciates this belief comes from Cromwell's military experience in the Civil War. Writing to William Lenthall a few days after his New Model Army had executed a victorious siege of the city of Bristol in 1645, he said:

> Presbyterians, Independents, all have here the same spirit of faith and prayer; the same presence and answer; they agree here, have no names of difference: pity it is it should be otherwise anywhere! All that believe, have the real unity, which is most glorious, because inward and spiritual, in the Body, and to the Head. As for being united in forms, commonly called Uniformity, every Christian will for peace-sake study and do, as far as conscience will permit; and from brethren in things of the mind we look for no compulsion, but that of light and reason.[34]

For Cromwell all believers possess a genuine unity because each is indwelt by the Spirit of God. This unity is the one that ultimately matters in the light of eternity for it speaks of union with the head of the church, namely Christ. Cromwell is not prepared to say that unity in external matters such as forms of worship and church government, so-called uniformity, is meaningless. These are matters about which Christians should pray for light and with regard to which they need to discuss and reason together. But, in Cromwell's mind, they are clearly not issues over which Christian brothers and sisters should divide.

The same emphasis on what another Puritan, Richard Baxter (1615–1691), called "mere

Christianity," re-appears during Cromwell's campaign in Scotland in 1650–1651. He was reluctant to enter into war against the Scots, because both they and the parliamentary armies shared the same Reformed faith.[35] Yet, he was utterly opposed to the Scottish Presbyterian exaltation of their distinctives as being the only option when it came to church government and their desire to coerce others by force into embracing them. Presbyterian or any form of church government, he told the Scots,

> are not by the Covenant to be imposed by force; yet we do and are ready to embrace so much as doth, or shall be made appear to us to be according to the Word of God. Are we to be dealt with as enemies, because we come not to your way? Is all religion wrapped up in that or any one form? Doth that name, or thing, give the difference between those that are the members of Christ and those that are not? We think not so. We say, faith working by love is the true character of a Christian; and, God is our witness, in whomsoever we see any thing of Christ to be, there we reckon our duty to love, waiting for a more plentiful effusion of the Spirit of God to make all those Christians, who, by the malice of the world, are diversified, and by their own carnal-mindedness, do diversify themselves by several names of reproach, to be of one heart and one mind, worshipping God with one consent.[36]

The Christian is called to love all in whom Christ dwells regardless of their denominational affiliation. After all, such denominational divisions, Cromwell feels, have their origin in worldliness and fleshly reasoning. Cromwell overlooks the fact that there are at times other, genuinely positive reasons for the development of differing ecclesial bodies. For instance, it is quite appropriate for godly congregations to leave a church connection that has abandoned the vital truths of the faith. But Cromwell is certainly correct in discerning that a significant amount of disagreement among genuine Christians is simply carnal narrow-mindedness. Waiting (and praying?) for an outpouring of the Spirit that will unify God's people in love is thus an essential aspect of Cromwellian spirituality. It is not without significance that among Cromwell's final words was a prayer for God to give his people "one heart and mutual love."[37]

Thus, when Cromwell was appointed Lord Protector in 1653, it is completely understandable that he sought to create a climate that would make room for the differences of conviction between professing Christians. Scholars differ as to the exact parameters of Cromwell's policy of religious toleration and all of the motives that guided him in this regard.[38] There is, however, little gainsaying the plain fact that Cromwell had a burning desire for an atmosphere of religious toleration that was far in advance of what most in his day were willing to sanction. One of the main reasons that he fought in the Civil War was to secure genuine religious liberty.[39] As he told Parliament in 1654:

> Is not Liberty of Conscience in religion a fundamental? So long as there is liberty of conscience for the supreme magistrate to exercise his conscience in erecting what form of church-government he is satisfied he should set up, why should not he give it to others? Liberty of conscience is a natural right... All the money of this nation would not have tempted men to fight upon such an account as they have engaged, if they had not had hopes of liberty, better than they had from Episcopacy, or than would have been afforded them from a Scottish Presbytery, or an English either...[40]

The one place that Cromwell drew the line with regard to religious liberty was where that liberty threatened the maintenance of public law and order.[41]

Probably the most amazing statement by Cromwell in favour of such a toleration is a remark that he made in 1652. He forthrightly declared that "he had rather that Mahometanism were permitted amongst us than that one of God's children should be persecuted."[42] Central to this declaration is the conviction that if unity between the various groups of Christians is not immediately possible, then a second best is liberty of conscience.[43] This statement also reveals, as Geoffrey F. Nuttall has noted, a sturdy faith in the might of the Holy Spirit to lead

Christian men and women of differing views into unity.[44] Thus Cromwell could write to the Presbyterian Governor of Edinburgh Castle, Walter Dundas, on September 12, 1650, with regard to Presbyterian fears for orthodoxy if freedom of conscience be allowed in religious matters:

> Your pretended fear lest error should step in, is like the man that would keep all the wine out of the country lest men should be drunk. It will be found an unjust and unwise jealousy, to deny a man the liberty he hath by nature upon a supposition that he may abuse it.[45]

In light of this central emphasis on Christian unity in Cromwell's spirituality it is somewhat ironic that his major religious legacy was the three denominations that emerged from the splintering of Puritanism in the latter half of the seventeenth century—the Presbyterians, Congregationalists (or Independents), and the Baptists, the so-called Nonconformists or Dissenters.[46] They did not have the depth of Cromwell's passion for Christian unity, but they did share Cromwell's providentialism, his emphasis on the new birth, and especially his interest in the work of the Holy Spirit in the life of the believer. These three groups, like Cromwell, had inherited from the continental Reformers of the sixteenth century, and from John Calvin (1506–1564) in particular, "a constant and even distinctive concern" with the person and work of the Holy Spirit.[47]

Benjamin B. Warfield (1851–1921), the distinguished American Presbyterian theologian, can actually speak of Calvin as "preeminently the theologian of the Holy Spirit."[48] Of his Puritan heirs, and Cromwell is to be included here, and their interest in the Spirit Warfield has this to say: "it is only the truth to say that Puritan thought was almost entirely occupied with loving study of the work of the Holy Spirit, and found its highest expression in dogmatico-practical expositions of the several aspects of it… For a century and a half afterward, indeed, this topic continued to form the hinge of the theologizing of the English Nonconformists."[49] In this way, Oliver Cromwell's spirituality, along with that of his fellow Puritans, made a lasting impact on the nature of English-speaking Evangelicalism and continued "to honour God" long after his death.

[1] Niall Ferguson, ed., *Virtual History: Alternatives and Counterfactuals* (London: Papermac, 1998), 91–124.
[2] *The Cousins' Wars: Religion, Politics and the Triumph of Anglo-America* (New York: Basic Books, 1999), 36–39.
[3] See p.90.
[4] "The Making of Oliver Cromwell" in John Morrill's *The Nature of the English Revolution* (London/New York: Longman, 1993), 118–147.
[5] Ibid., 118.
[6] J.C. Davis, "Cromwell's religion" in John Morrill, *Oliver Cromwell and the English Revolution* (London/New York: Longman, 1990), 190–191.
[7] *Of the Providence of God* [*The Works of Richard Sibbes*, ed. Alexander B. Grosart (1862–1864 ed.; repr. Edinburgh: The Banner of Truth Trust, 1977), V, 35]. For this reference, I am

indebted to Blair Worden, "Providence and Politics in Cromwellian England," *Past & Present*, 109 (November 1985), 60, an article that has been very helpful in understanding Cromwell's convictions about providence. Also helpful in this regard are H.F. Lovell Cocks, *The Religious Life of Oliver Cromwell* (London: Independent Press Ltd., 1960), 28–44, and Davis, "Cromwell's religion," 186–188, 199–201.
[8] See p.117.
[9] See p.75.
[10] See pp.51,53. For further examples, see p.69; Worden, "Providence and Politics," 67–70, 81–83.
[11] Thomas Carlyle, *Oliver Cromwell's Letters and Speeches with Elucidations* (New York: Charles Scribner's Sons, 1897), III, 189. It was victories such as these that led the Puritan divine John Owen (1616–1683), one of Cromwell's trusted advisers, to tell him in 1654: "The series and chain of eminent providences whereby you have been carried on and protected in all the hazardous work of your generation, which your God hath called you unto, is evident to all." Quoted from *The Doctrine of the Saints' Perseverance Explained and Confirmed* [*The Works of John Owen*, ed. William H. Goold (1850–1853 ed.; repr. Edinburgh: The Banner of Truth Trust, 1981), XI, 5].
[12] See *Diary of Thomas Burton, Esq.*, ed. John Towill Rutt (London: Henry Colburn, 1828), I, xxx; Geoffrey F. Nuttall, *The Puritan Spirit* (London: Epworth Press, 1967), 130–136.
[13] Cited Nuttall, *Puritan Spirit*, 134, n.1. See also Johann Sommerville, "Oliver Cromwell and English Political Thought" in Morrill, ed., *Oliver Cromwell and the English Revolution*, 252–253.
[14] Barry Coward, *Cromwell* (London/New York: Longman, 1991), 10–12; Morrill, "Making of Oliver Cromwell," 119–123.
[15] See, for instance, Robert S. Paul, *The Lord Protector: Religion and Politics in the Life of Oliver Cromwell* (Grand Rapids: William B. Eerdmans, 1955), 24–27.
[16] Morrill, "Making of Oliver Cromwell," 126–130.

[17] Ibid., 134.
[18] Ibid., 134–135. For the date, see Paul, *Lord Protector*, 38–41; Morrill, "Making of Oliver Cromwell," 134–135.
[19] See p.47–48. The best analysis of this text is Paul, *Lord Protector*, 37–38.
[20] For the citations and allusions to Scripture, see p.48–49.
[21] Morrill, "Making of Oliver Cromwell," 134.
[22] Davis, "Cromwell's religion," 187.
[23] See p.65.
[24] See p.91.
[25] Ibid.
[26] See p.92.
[27] See p.112.
[28] See pp.85,87.
[29] See p.63.
[30] See pp.111–112.
[31] See p.63.
[32] See p.51.
[33] Davis, "Cromwell's religion," 191.
[34] See p.57.
[35] See pp.82–83, n.3. See also Coward, *Cromwell*, 76–78.
[36] See pp.81–82. Cromwell could be just as critical of the Calvinistic Baptists when they tried something similar. See pp.113–115.
[37] See p.129. For a further discussion of this theme, a discussion that is not without its problems, see Davis, "Cromwell's religion," 201–207.
[38] See, for instance, Paul, *Lord Protector*, 324–333; Cocks, *Religious Life of Oliver Cromwell*, 45–63; George A. Drake, "Oliver Cromwell and the Quest for Religious Toleration" in Jerald C. Brauer, ed., *The Impact of the Church Upon Its Culture* (Chicago: The University of Chicago Press, 1968), 267–291; Roger Howell, Jr., "Cromwell and English Liberty" in R.C. Richardson and G.M. Ridden, eds., *Freedom and the English Revolution. Essays in History and Literature* (Manchester: Manchester University Press, 1986), 25–44;

Blair Worden, "Toleration and the Cromwellian Protectorate" in W.J. Sheils, ed., *Persecution and Toleration* (Oxford: Basil Blackwell for the Ecclesiastical History Society, 1984), 199–233; Davis, "Cromwell's religion," 191–199.

[39] Howell, "Cromwell and English Liberty," 28.

[40] See pp.105–106.

[41] Howell, "Cromwell and English Liberty," 30.

[42] Cited Geoffrey F. Nuttall, *The Holy Spirit in Puritan Faith and Experience* (2nd. ed.; Oxford: Basil Blackwell, 1947), 127.

[43] Davis, "Cromwell's religion," 198–199.

[44] *Holy Spirit in Puritan Faith and Experience*, 127. See also pp.81–82.

[45] Carlyle, *Oliver Cromwell's Letters and Speeches*, II, 235.

[46] Coward, *Cromwell*, 176–177.

[47] Richard B. Gaffin, "The Holy Spirit," *The Westminster Theological Journal*, 43 (1980) 61. See also the detailed discussion by Garth B. Wilson, "Doctrine of the Holy Spirit in the Reformed Tradition: A Critical Overview," in George Vandervelde, ed., *The Holy Spirit: Renewing and Empowering Presence* (Winfield, British Columbia: Wood Lake Books, 1989), 57–62.

[48] "Calvin's Doctrine of the Knowledge of God" in Samuel G. Craig, ed., *Calvin and Augustine* (Repr. Phillipsburg, New Jersey: Presbyterian and Reformed Publishing Co., 1980) 107. See also "John Calvin: The Man and His Work" and "John Calvin the Theologian," in ibid., 21, 487.

[49] "Introductory Note" to Abraham Kuyper, *The Work of the Holy Spirit* (1900 ed.; repr. Grand Rapids Wm. B. Eerdmans Publ. Co., 1956), xxviii.

Chronology

1599

April 25—Oliver Cromwell is born in Huntingdon

1616

Studies at Sidney Sussex College, Cambridge

1617

June—Cromwell's father dies; Cromwell leaves Cambridge and returns home

1620

August 2—Cromwell marries Elizabeth Bourchier

1628

Elected MP for Huntingdon

1640

Elected MP for Cambridge

1642

August 2—The Civil War begins. Cromwell raises a troop of cavalry at Huntingdon

1644

Appointed lieutenant-general

July 2—Parliamentary victory at Marston Moor

1645

June 10—Parliamentary victory at Naseby

1646

May—End of the first phase of the Civil War

1647

October 28–November 8—Putney Debates

1648

Second phase of the Civil War begins

August 17—Defeat of the Scots at the Battle of Preston

1649

January—The trial and execution of Charles I

August—Cromwell sails to Ireland

September—The sack of Drogheda

1650

September 3—Cromwellian victory at the Battle of Dunbar

1651

September 3—Victory for Cromwell at the Battle of Worcester. End of the second phase of the Civil War

1653

December 12—Cromwell becomes Lord Protector

1655

War against Spain

December—Re-admission of the Jews to England discussed

1656

October–December—The case of James Naylor

1657

June 26—Second installation as Lord Protector

1658

August 6—Death of Cromwell's daughter, Elizabeth Claypole

September 3—Death of Oliver Cromwell

1661

January 30—Cromwell's body, disinterred from Westminster Abbey, is hung on the gallows at Tyburn and then cast into an unmarked grave

1

To my very loving Friend Mr. Storie [1]

St. Ives, January 11, 1635

Mr. Storie,

Amongst the catalogue of those good works which your fellow-citizens and our countrymen have done, this will not be reckoned for the least, that they have provided for the feeding of souls. Building of hospitals provides for men's bodies; to build material temples is judged a work of piety; but they that procure spiritual food, they that build up spiritual temples, they are the men truly charitable, truly pious. Such a work as this was your erecting the lecture in our country; in the which you placed Dr. Welles, a man of goodness and industry, and ability to do good every way, not short of any I know in England;[2] and I am persuaded that, sithence[3] his coming, the Lord hath by him wrought much good amongst us.

It only remains now that he who first moved you to this, put you forward to the continuance thereof; it was the Lord, and therefore to him lift we up our hearts that he would perfect it. And surely, Mr.

Storie, it were a piteous thing to see a lecture fall, in the hands of so many able and godly men as I am persuaded the founders of this are, in these times, wherein we see they are suppressed, with too much haste and violence by the enemies of God [and] his truth. Far be it that so much guilt should stick to your hands, who live in a city so renowned for the clear shining light of the gospel.[4] You know, Mr. Storie, to withdraw the pay is to let fall the lecture; for who goeth to warfare at his own cost?[5] I beseech you therefore in the bowels of Christ Jesus put it forward, and let the good man have his pay. The souls of God's children will bless you for it; and so shall I…

1 Thomas Carlyle, *Oliver Cromwell's Letters and Speeches with Elucidations* (New York: Charles Scribner's Sons, 1897), I, 89–90. "Mr. Storie" is probably George Storie, a resident of London, who had strong New England ties and was inclined towards Puritanism. St. Ives, Cambridgeshire, is about twelve miles north-west of Cambridge. Cromwell lived at St. Ives from 1630 to 1636.

2 "Dr. Welles" is usually identified with Samuel Wells (1614–1678), a Puritan minister who pastored mostly in Oxfordshire. As John Morrill has shown, however, this individual is probably Dr. Walter Welles, lecturer in Godmanchester, half a mile from Huntington. See Morrill, "The Making of Oliver Cromwell" in his *The Nature of the English Revolution* (London/New York: Longman, 1993), 138–139. The lectureship to which Cromwell refers in this letter was a means whereby a Puritan congregation could ensure that it received biblical teaching. Funds would be collected by the congregation to pay for a lecturer, who might

or might not be the minister of the church. If the minister's sermons were to the taste of the congregation, the funds were paid to him. If not, a lecturer from outside would be paid to give the congregation biblical exposition. The leadership in the Church of England sought to suppress these lectureships and thus curtail the growth of Puritanism. Cromwell's support of them clearly indicates his theological affinities.

[3] An obsolete word that in this context has the meaning of "since."

[4] At this point in time London had a goodly number of Puritan preachers.

[5] 1 Corinthians 9:7 (Geneva version).

2

To my beloved Cousin Mrs. St. John [1]

Ely, October 13, 1638

Dear Cousin,

I thankfully acknowledge your love in your kind remembrance of me upon this opportunity. Alas, you do too highly prize my lines, and my company. I may be ashamed to own your expressions, considering how unprofitable I am, and the mean improvement of my talent.

Yet to honour my God by declaring what he hath done for my soul, in this I am confident, and I will be so. Truly, then, this I find: That he giveth springs in a dry and barren wilderness where no water is.[2] I live (you know where) in Mesheck, which they say signifies *Prolonging*; in Kedar, which signifies *Blackness*:[3] yet the Lord forsaketh me not. Though he do prolong, yet he will I trust bring me to his tabernacle, to his resting-place. My soul is with the congregation of the firstborn,[4] my body rests in hope, and if here I may honour my God either by doing or by suffering, I shall be most glad.

Truly no poor creature hath more cause to put forth himself in the cause of his God than I. I have had plentiful wages beforehand, and I am sure I shall never earn the least mite. The Lord accept me in his Son, and give me to walk in the light,—and give us to walk in the light, as he is the light![5] He it is that enlighteneth our blackness, our darkness.[6] I dare not say, he hideth his face from me. He giveth me to see light in his light.[7] One beam in a dark place hath exceeding much refreshment in it:—blessed be his name for shining upon so dark a heart as mine! You know what my manner of life hath been. Oh, I lived in and loved darkness, and hated the light. I was a chief, the chief of sinners.[8] This is true; I hated godliness, yet God had mercy on me. O the riches of his mercy! Praise him for me;—pray for me, that he who hath begun a good work would perfect it to the day of Christ.[9]

1 Carlyle, *Oliver Cromwell's Letters and Speeches*, I, 100–101. Elizabeth St. John was Cromwell's cousin and the wife of Oliver St. John (*c.*1598–1673), who served as Lord Chief Justice during the Commonwealth. Ely, Cambridgeshire, is about fifteen miles north-east of Cambridge.

This letter provides an essential insight into the spiritual foundation of Cromwell's subsequent life. His conversion would have taken place about eight or nine years before this letter. As the following footnotes indicate, it is interlaced with biblical quotes and phrases. For a listing of all of the biblical phrases in the letter, see Robert S. Paul, *The Lord Protector: Religion and Politics in the Life of Oliver Cromwell* (Grand Rapids: William B. Eerdmans, 1955), 37, 399–400.

2 Psalm 63:1.

3 Psalm 120:5.

4 Hebrews 12:23 (Geneva version).

[5] Compare 1 John 1:7.
[6] Compare 2 Samuel 22:29.
[7] Compare Psalm 36:9.
[8] 1 Timothy 1:15.
[9] Philippians 1:6.

3

To Colonel Valentine Walton [1]

July 5, 1644

Dear Sir,

It's our duty to sympathise in all mercies; that we may praise the Lord together in chastisements or trials, that so we may sorrow together.

...Truly England and the Church of God hath had a great favour from the Lord, in this great victory given unto us, such as the like never was since this war began. ...Give glory, all the glory, to God.

Sir, God hath taken away your eldest son by a cannon-shot. It brake his leg. We were necessitated to have it cut off, whereof he died.

Sir, you know my trials this way;[2] but the Lord supported me with this, that the Lord took him into the happiness we all pant after and live for. There is your precious child full of glory, to know sin nor sorrow any more. He was a gallant young man, exceeding gracious. God give you his comfort. ...he was a precious young man, fit for God. You have cause to bless the Lord. He is a glorious saint in heaven, wherein you ought exceedingly to rejoice. Let this drink up your sorrow; seeing these are not feigned words to comfort you, but the thing is so real and undoubted a truth. You may do all things by the strength of Christ.[3] Seek that, and you shall easily bear your trial.

1 Carlyle, *Oliver Cromwell's Letters and Speeches*, I, 187–189. This letter was written shortly after the Battle of Marston Moor on July 2, 1644. Valentine Walton (died *c.*1661) was Cromwell's brother-in-law. His son, of whom Cromwell writes in this letter, was also named Valentine. He was thus Cromwell's nephew.

2 This is a reference to the deaths of Cromwell's two eldest sons: Robert (1621–1639), who died of unspecified causes, and Oliver, Jr. (1623–1644), who had succumbed to smallpox at Newport Pagnell, a few months before the Battle of Marston Moor.

3 Philippians 4:13. Only a short time before his own death in 1658, Cromwell mentioned how important this biblical text was to him. "This Scripture," he said, "did once save my life, when my eldest Son died, which went as a dagger to my heart, indeed it did" (Carlyle, *Oliver Cromwell's Letters and Speeches*, IV, 198). For a sermonic study of Philippians 4:13 as Cromwell's life verse, see Frank W. Boreham, *A Bunch of Everlastings, or, Texts that Made History* (6th ed.; London: Epworth Press, 1955), 77–84.

4

For the Honourable William Lenthall [1]

[Market] Harborough, June 14, 1645

...Sir, this is none other but the hand of God; and to him alone belongs the glory, wherein none are to share with him. The General served you with all faithfulness and honour; and the best commendation I can give him is, that I dare say he attributes all to God, and would rather perish than assume to himself.[2] Which is an honest and a thriving way, and yet as much for bravery may be given to him, in this action, as to a man. Honest men served you faithfully in this action. Sir, they are trusty; I beseech you in the name of God, not to discourage them. I wish this action may beget thankfulness and humility in all that are concerned in it. He that ventures his life for the liberty of his country, I wish he trust God for the liberty of his conscience, and you for the liberty he fights for.

[1] Carlyle, *Oliver Cromwell's Letters and Speeches*, I, 214–215. William Lenthall (1591–1662) was the Speaker of the House of Commons throughout what is known as the Long

Sr. beinge comanded by you to this
seruice, I thinke my selfe bound to ac=
quaint you with the good hand of God
towards you, and vs, wee marched yesterday
after the Kinge, whoe went before vs
from Dauentree to Haurebrowe, and quar
tered about six miles from him, this day
wee marched towards him, Hee drew out
to meete vs, both Armies engaged, wee,
after 3 howers fight, very doubtfull
att last routed his Armie, killed and
tooke about 5000. very many officers
but of what quallitye wee yett know
not; wee tooke alsoe about 200. carrag
all hee had, and all his gunns, beinge
12. in number, whereof 2. were Demi
canon, 2 demie Culueringes, and (I
thinke) the rest Sacres, wee pursued
the enimie from three miles short of Ha
to nine beyond, euen to sight of Leic
whether the Kinge fled. Sr this is non
other but the hand of God, and to him
aloane belongs the Glorie, wherein no
are to share with him, The Generall
serued you with all faythfullnesse an
honor, and the best comendations I can
giue him is, that I dare say hee

attributes all to God, and would rather perish then assume to himselfe, which is an honest, and a thriueinge way, and yett as much for brauery may bee giuen to him in this action as to a man. Honest men serued you faythfully in this action, Sr they are trusty, I beseech you in the name of God not to discourage them, I wish this action may begett thankfullnesse and humilitye in all that are concerned in it, Hee that ventures his life for the libertye of his countrie, I wish hee trust God for the libertye of his conscience, and you for the libertye hee fights for, In this hee rests whoe is

Your most humble seruant
Oliver Cromwell

June 14th 1645.
Haurebrowe.

Oliver Cromwell's letter to William Lenthall on June 14, 1645

[Reproduced from a nineteenth century reproduction of the manuscript which is in the British Library]

Parliament, which met from 1640 to 1648. This letter was written on the day of the Battle of Naseby. Market Harborough is about five miles from the battlefield.

[2] i.e. Thomas Fairfax. On Fairfax, see pp.59–61.

5

For the Honourable William Lenthall [1]

Bristol, September 14, 1645

...Sir, they that have been employed in this service[2] know that faith and prayer obtained this city for you. I do not say ours only, but of the people of God with you and all England over, who have wrestled with God for a blessing in this very thing. Our desires are, that God may be glorified by the same spirit of faith by which we ask all our sufficiency, and having received it, it's meet that he have all the praise. Presbyterians, Independents,[3] all have here the same spirit of faith and prayer; the same presence and answer; they agree here, have no names of difference: pity it is it should be otherwise anywhere! All that believe, have the real unity, which is most glorious, because inward and spiritual, in the Body, and to the Head. As for being united in forms, commonly called Uniformity, every Christian will for peace-sake study and do, as far as conscience will permit; and from brethren in things of the mind we look for no compulsion, but that of light and reason.

[1] Carlyle, *Oliver Cromwell's Letters and Speeches*, I, 228. This letter was written a few days after the victorious siege of Bristol by the parliamentary army.
[2] i.e. fighting at the siege of Bristol.
[3] The term "Independents" was regularly used during the seventeenth and eighteenth centuries to refer to the body now known as "Congregationalists."

6

For his Excellency Sir Thomas Fairfax [1]

March 7, 1646

Sir,

It hath pleased God to raise me out of a dangerous sickness; and I do most willingly acknowledge that the Lord hath (in this visitation) exercised the bowels of a Father towards me. I received in myself the sentence of death, that I might learn to trust in him that raiseth from the dead, and have no confidence in the flesh.[2] It's a blessed thing to die daily. For what is there in this world to be accounted of! The best men according to the flesh, and things, are lighter than vanity. I find this only good, to love the Lord and his poor despised people, to do for them, and to be ready to suffer with them:…and he that is found worthy of this hath obtained great favour from the Lord; and he that is established in this shall (being conformed to Christ and the rest of the Body[3]) participate in the glory of a resurrection which will answer all.

Thomas Fairfax

[From the painting by Gerard Zoust. Reproduced from the frontispiece of Thomas Carlyle, *Oliver Cromwell's Letters and Speeches with Elucidations* (New York: Charles Scribner's Sons, 1897), III]

[1] Carlyle, *Oliver Cromwell's Letters and Speeches*, I, 302–303. Carlyle places the date of this letter in 1647. I have followed the dating of Abbott (*The Writings and Speeches of Oliver Cromwell*, I, 429, n.77). Thomas Fairfax (1612–1671) was a professional soldier and the commander-in-chief of the parliamentary armies until 1650. He genuinely sought religious reformation, but was opposed to the political and social changes that took place during the Commonwealth. He played a key role in the restoration of the monarchy in 1660.

[2] 2 Corinthians 1:9.

[3] i.e. the Body of Christ, his Church.

7

For my beloved Daughter Bridget Ireton [1]

London, October 25, 1646

Dear Daughter,

...Your Sister Claypole[2] is, I trust in mercy, exercised with some perplexed thoughts. She sees her own vanity and carnal mind, bewailing it; she seeks after (as I hope also) that which will satisfy. And thus to be a seeker is to be of the best sect next to a finder; and such an one shall every faithful humble seeker be at the end. Happy seeker, happy finder! Who ever tasted that the Lord is gracious,[3] without some sense of self, vanity, and badness? Who ever tasted that graciousness of his, and could go less[4] in desire, and less in pressing after full enjoyment? Dear Heart, press on; let not husband, let not anything cool thy affections after Christ. I hope he will be an occasion to inflame them. That which is best worthy of love in thy husband is that of the image of Christ he bears. Look on that, and love it best, and all the rest for that. I pray for thee and him; do so for me.

[1] Carlyle, *Oliver Cromwell's Letters and Speeches*, I, 254–255. Bridget Cromwell (1624–1662) was Cromwell's eldest daughter. She had married Henry Ireton (1611–1651), one of Cromwell's closest confidants, in June 1646. Ireton was an important parliamentary general and political theorist who played a vital role in most of the key battles of the Civil War.

[2] Elizabeth Claypole (1629–1658) was Cromwell's second oldest daughter. In the January of the same year that saw Bridget married to Henry Ireton, Elizabeth had married John Claypole, Jr. (*c.*1625–1688), who eventually became Cromwell's Master of the Horse. Elizabeth's temperament was quite different from that of Bridget. Whereas Bridget was greatly exercised about the state of her soul, Elizabeth was given to frivolity and even flights of vanity. See Antonia Fraser, *Cromwell: Our Chief of Men* (London: Weidenfeld and Nicolson, 1973), 173–174, 177–178. This would account for Cromwell's remarks about Elizabeth in this letter.

[3] Compare Psalm 34:8.

[4] i.e. "could become less."

8

For my worthy Friend Oliver St. John, Esquire [1]

Knaresborough, September 1, [1648]

Dear Sir,

I can say nothing but surely the Lord our God is a great and glorious God. He only is worthy to be feared and trusted, and his appearances patiently to be waited for. He will not fail his people. Let every thing that hath breath praise the Lord.[2]

Remember my love to my dear brother H. Vane.[3] I pray he make not too little, nor I too much, of outward dispensations. God preserve us all, that we, in simplicity of our spirits, may patiently attend upon them. Let us all not be careful what use men will make of these actings. They shall, will they, nill they,[4] fulfil the good pleasure of God, and so shall serve our generations. Our rest we expect elsewhere; that will be durable. Care we not for tomorrow, nor for anything. This Scripture has been of great stay to me; read it: Isaiah 8:10,11,14—read all the chapter.[5]

[1] Carlyle, *Oliver Cromwell's Letters and Speeches*, I, 358. Knaresborough is about sixteen miles north of Leeds.

[2] Psalm 150:6.

[3] Henry Vane the Younger (1613–1662) was a close friend of Cromwell during the Civil War. An advocate of radical republicanism, he broke with Cromwell in the 1650s since he felt Cromwell was acquiring too much power.

[4] "Nill" as a verb has the archaic meaning of "to be unwilling." Cromwell's point here is that whatever men might plan, God's purposes will go forward and be fulfilled.

[5] Isaiah 8 is an encouragement to seek wisdom from God, heed his Word, and cultivate a fear of him. Isaiah 8:10–11, 13–14 run thus in the King James version: "Take counsel together, and it shall come to nought; speak the word, and it shall not stand: for God *is* with us. For the Lord spake thus to me with a strong hand, and instructed me that I should not walk in the way of this people… Sanctify the Lord of hosts himself; and *let* him *be* your fear, and *let* him *be* your dread. And he shall be for a sanctuary; but for a stone of stumbling and for a rock of offence to both the houses of Israel, for a gin and for a snare to the inhabitants of Jerusalem."

9

For the Right Honourable the Lord Wharton [1]

September 2, 1648

My Lord,

You know how untoward I am at this business of writing, yet a word. I beseech the Lord make us sensible of this great mercy here...[2] I trust [to have, through] the goodness of our God, time and opportunity to speak of it to you face to face. When we think of our God, what are we? Oh, his mercy to the whole society of saints, despised, jeered saints! Let them mock on. Would we were all saints. The best of us are, God knows, poor weak saints, yet saints; if not sheep, yet lambs, and must be fed. We have daily bread,[3] and shall have it, in despite of all enemies. There's enough in our Father's house, and he dispenseth it... I think, through these outward mercies (as we call them), faith, patience, love, hope, all are exercised and perfected, yea, Christ formed, and grows to a perfect man within us. I know not how well to distinguish, the difference is only in the subject. To a worldly man they are outward, to a saint Christian... [4]

[1] Carlyle, *Oliver Cromwell's Letters and Speeches*, I, 361. Philip Wharton (1613–1696), the fourth Lord Wharton, was first and foremost a Puritan, whose public life was shaped by his theological convictions. Active in opposing the King during the Civil War, he disagreed with the execution of Charles I, and withdrew from politics for the duration of the Commonwealth. After the restoration of the monarchy he was a strong supporter of the Nonconformist cause.
[2] This "mercy" is the parliamentary victory over the Scots at the Battle of Preston on August 17, 1648.
[3] i.e. spiritual food.
[4] Cromwell appears to be arguing that the same events have different results in the lives of various people, depending on whether or not they are Christians.

10

To Colonel Robert Hammond [1]

November 25, 1648

Dear Robin,

...Thou desirest to hear of my experiences. I can tell thee. I am such a one as thou didst formerly know, having a body of sin and death,[2] but I thank God, through Jesus Christ our Lord there is no condemnation, though much infirmity, and I wait for the redemption.[3] And in this poor condition I obtain mercy,[4] and sweet consolation through the Spirit, and find abundant cause every day to exalt the Lord, and abase flesh, and herein I have some exercise.

As to outward dispensations, if we may so call them, we have not been without our share of beholding some remarkable providences, and appearances of the Lord.[5] His presence hath been amongst us, and by the light of his countenance we have prevailed.[6] We are sure the good-will of him who dwelt in the bush has shined upon us,[7] and we can humbly say, We know in whom we have believed,[8] who is able and will perfect what remaineth, and us also in doing what is well-pleasing in his eyesight.[9]

I find some trouble in your spirit; occasioned

first, not only by the continuance of your sad and heavy burden, as you call it, upon you, but by the dissatisfaction you take at the ways of some good men whom you love with your heart…

To the first: call not your burden sad or heavy. If your Father laid it upon you, he intended neither. He is the Father of lights, from whom comes every good and perfect gift, who of his own will begot us,[10] and bade us count it all joy when such things befall us, they being for the exercise of faith and patience, whereby in the end we shall be made perfect (James 1).[11]

Dear Robin, our fleshly reasonings ensnare us.[12] These make us say, heavy, sad, pleasant, easy. Was there not a little of this when Robert Hammond, through dissatisfaction too, desired retirement from the Army, and thought of quiet in the Isle of Wight? Did not God find him out there? I believe he will never forget this. And now I perceive he is to seek again; partly through his sad and heavy burden, and partly through his dissatisfaction with friends' actings.

Dear Robin, thou and I were never worthy to be door-keepers in this service.[13] If thou wilt seek, seek to know the mind of God in all that chain of Providence, whereby God brought thee thither, and that person to thee;[14] how before and since, God has ordered him, and affairs concerning him; and then tell me, whether there be not some glorious and high meaning in all this, above what thou hast yet attained? And laying aside thy fleshly reason, seek of the Lord to teach thee what that is; and he will do it. I dare be positive to say, it is not that the wicked should be exalted, that God should so appear as indeed he hath done. For there is no peace to them.[15] No, it is set upon the hearts of such as fear the Lord, and we have witness upon witness, that it shall go ill with them and their partakers. I say again, seek that Spirit to teach thee, which is the spirit of knowledge and understanding, the spirit of counsel and might, of wisdom and of the fear of the Lord.[16] That spirit will close thine eyes and stop thine ears, so that thou shalt not judge by them, but thou shalt judge for the meek of the earth,[17] and thou shalt be made able to do accordingly. The Lord direct thee to that which is well-pleasing in his eyesight.[18]

1 Carlyle, *Oliver Cromwell's Letters and Speeches*, I, 401–403. Robert Hammond (1621–1654) saw action in a number of engagements during the Civil War. In 1647 he was appointed Governor of the Isle of Wight. For a year, from November 1647 to November of 1648, he acted as the jailer of Charles I, as the king was sequestered on the island. He maintained a close relationship to Cromwell, and the latter would have employed his services widely during his Protectorate if Hammond had not died of a fever in Ireland in October 1654.

2 Romans 6:6.

3 Compare Romans 8:21–25.

4 1 Timothy 1:13.

5 Among "those remarkable providences" would be the Battle of Preston on August 17, 1648.

6 Psalm 44:3.

7 Exodus 3:1–6; Deuteronomy 33:16.

[8] 2 Timothy 1:12.
[9] Hebrews 13:21.
[10] James 1:17–18.
[11] Compare James 1:2–6.
[12] 2 Corinthians 1:12.
[13] Psalm 84:10.
[14] i.e. King Charles I.
[15] Isaiah 57:21.
[16] Isaiah 11:2.
[17] Isaiah 11:4.
[18] Hebrews 13:21.

11

To my beloved Daughter Dorothy Cromwell[1]

From aboard the John
August 13, 1649

My dear Daughter,

Your letter was very welcome to me. I like to see anything from your hand, because indeed I stick not to say[2] I do entirely love you. And therefore I hope a word of advice will not be unwelcome nor unacceptable to thee.

I desire you both to make it above all things your business to seek the Lord: to be frequently calling upon him, that he would manifest himself to you in his Son, and be listening what returns he makes to you, for he will be speaking in your ear and in your heart, if you attend thereunto. I desire you to provoke your husband likewise thereunto. As for the pleasures of this life, and outward business, let that be upon the bye. Be above all these things, by faith in Christ; and then you shall have the true use and comfort of them, and not otherwise. I have much satisfaction in hope your spirit is this way set; and I desire you may grow in grace, and in the knowledge of our Lord and Saviour Jesus Christ, and that I may hear thereof. The Lord is very near, which we see by his wonderful works, and therefore he looks that we of this generation draw near to him....

The Lord bless thee, my dear daughter.

[1] Carlyle, *Oliver Cromwell's Letters and Speeches*, II, 43–44. Dorothy Cromwell (1628–1676) was the wife of Cromwell's third son, Richard (1626–1712), who succeeded his father as Lord Protector. Dorothy was the eldest daughter of Richard Maijor (1604–1660) of Hursley, Hampshire, a prosperous landowner. For an extract from a letter to Maijor, see the following text. This letter to Dorothy was written on board the ship *John*, as Cromwell was preparing to sail for Ireland. It would be during this campaign in Ireland that Cromwell's reputation would be sullied by the sack of Drogheda. On this sack, see especially the judicious treatment by Paul, *Lord Protector*, 207–218, and Fraser, *Cromwell: Our Chief of Men*, 332–340, 355–357. See also the most recent study of Cromwell's campaign in Ireland by Tom Reilly, *Cromwell—An Honourable Enemy* (Dingle, Co. Kerry: Brandon Publishing, 1999).

[2] In what is now a rare use of the word "stick," Cromwell is saying that he does not hesitate or scruple to tell his daughter-in-law of his love for her.

12

For my very loving Brother, Richard Maijor, Esquire [1]

Carrick, April 2, 1650

Dear Brother,

For me to write unto you the state of our affairs here were more than indeed I have leisure well to do, and therefore I hope you do not expect it from me, seeing when I write to the Parliament I usually am, as becomes me, very particular with them, and usually from thence the knowledge thereof is spread.

Only this let me say, which is the best intelligence to friends that are truly Christian: The Lord is pleased still to vouchsafe us his presence, and to prosper his own work in our hands, which to us is the more eminent because truly we are a company of poor, weak and worthless creatures. Truly our work is neither from our brains nor from our courage and strength, but we follow the Lord who goeth before, and gather what he scattereth, that so all may appear to be from him.

...If God be for us, who can be against us? Who can fight against the Lord and prosper? Who can resist his will? The Lord keep us in his love.

I desire your prayers; your family is often in mine. I rejoice to hear how it hath pleased the Lord to deal with my daughter.[2] The Lord bless her, and sanctify all his dispensations to them and us. I have committed my son to you; I pray counsel him.[3] Some letters I have lately had from him have a good savour; the Lord treasure up grace there, that out of that treasury he may bring forth good things.

1 Carlyle, *Oliver Cromwell's Letters and Speeches*, II, 159–160. This letter was written from Carrick, Ireland.

2 Dorothy Cromwell had given birth to a daughter on March 26, 1650.

3 Richard was living the life of a country squire at Hursley, where Maijor also lived.

13

For my beloved Son Richard Cromwell, Esquire[1]

Carrick, April 2, 1650

Dick Cromwell,

I take your letters kindly: I like expressions when they come plainly from the heart, and are not strained nor affected.

...Seek the Lord and his face continually: let this be the business of your life and strength, and let all things be subservient and in order to this. You cannot find nor behold the face of God but in Christ; therefore labour to know God in Christ, which the Scripture makes to be the sum of all, even life eternal.[2] Because the true knowledge is not literal or speculative; but inward, transforming the mind to it. It's uniting to, and participating of, the divine nature (2 Peter 1:4). It's such a knowledge as Paul speaks of (Philippians 3:8–10). How little of this knowledge of Christ is there among us. My weak prayers shall be for you.

Take heed of an unactive vain Spirit. Recreate yourself with Sir Walter Raughleye's [i.e. Raleigh's] History; it's a body of history, and will add much more to your understanding than fragments of story.[3]

...You will think, perhaps, I need not advise you to love your wife. The Lord teach you how to do it; or else it will be done ill-favouredly. Though marriage be no instituted Sacrament, yet where the undefiled bed is, and love, this union aptly resembles [that of] Christ and his Church. If you can truly love your wife, what [love] doth Christ bear to his Church and every poor soul therein, who gave himself for it and to it. Commend me to your wife; tell her I entirely love her, and rejoice in the goodness of the Lord to her. I wish her everyway fruitful.

1 Carlyle, *Oliver Cromwell's Letters and Speeches*, II, 161–162.

2 See 1 John 5:20.

3 *The History of the World* by Walter Raleigh (1552–1618) was a favourite with Puritans like Cromwell because of its providential view of history.

14

For my very loving Brother Richard Maijor, Esquire [1]

Alnwick, July 17, 1650

Dear Brother,

...I hope you give my son good counsel; I believe he needs it. He is in the dangerous time of his age, and it's a very vain world. O, how good it is to close with Christ betimes; there is nothing else worth the looking after. I beseech you call upon him. I hope you will discharge my duty and your own love; you see how I am employed. I need pity. I know what I feel. Great place and business in the world is not worth the looking after; I should have no comfort in mine but that my hope is in the Lord's presence. I have not sought these things; truly I have been called unto them by the Lord, and therefore am not without some assurance that he will enable his poor worm and weak servant to do his will, and to fulfil my generation. In this I beg your prayers.

[1] Carlyle, *Oliver Cromwell's Letters and Speeches*, II, 178.

Richard Cromwell

[From a drawing by W. Bond. Reproduced from Charles Firth, *Oliver Cromwell and the Rule of the Puritans in England* (London: G.P. Putnam's Sons, 1900)]

15

A Declaration of the Army of England upon their March into Scotland To all that are Saints, and partakers of the faith of God's Elect, in Scotland [1]

July 19, 1650

As for the Presbyterian, or any other form of church-government, they are not by the Covenant to be imposed by force; yet we do and are ready to embrace so much as doth, or shall be made appear to us to be according to the Word of God. Are we to be dealt with as enemies, because we come not to your way? Is all religion wrapped up in that or any one form? Doth that name, or thing, give the difference between those that are the members of Christ and those that are not? We think not so. We say, faith working by love[2] is the true character of a Christian; and, God is our witness, in whomsoever we see any thing of Christ to be, there we reckon our duty to love, waiting for a more plentiful effusion of the Spirit of God to make all those Christians, who, by the malice of the world, are diversified, and by their own carnal-mindedness, do diversify themselves by several names of reproach, to be of one heart and one mind, worshipping God with one consent. We are desirous that those who are for the Presbyterian government, should have all freedom to enjoy it; and are persuaded that if it be so much of God, as some affirm, if God be trusted with his own means, which is his Word powerfully and effectually preached, without a too-busy meddling with, or engaging, the authorities of the world, it is able to accomplish his good pleasure upon the minds of men, to produce and establish his purposes in the world, concerning the government of his church.[3]

[1] Wilbur Cortez Abbott with Catherine D. Crane, *The Writings and Speeches of Oliver Cromwell* (Cambridge: Harvard University Press, 1939), II, 285–286. During the second phase of the Civil War, which lasted from 1648 to 1651, the Scots, who had fought with the parliamentary armies during the first phase of the war from 1642 to 1646, took the side of the Stuart monarchy. Cromwell and his army invaded Scotland in July 1650. This passage is from a much longer text that seeks to convince the Scots that they and the English share a common Reformed heritage, and that therefore they should not be meeting as enemies on the battlefield.

[2] Galatians 5:6.

[3] Almost identical sentiments can be found in a letter Cromwell wrote to William Lenthall a couple of months later on September 4, 1650, the day after the Battle of Dunbar. Cromwell wrote: "Since we came in Scotland, it hath been our desire and longing to have avoided blood in

this business, by reason that God hath a people here fearing his name, though deceived. And to that end have we offered much love unto such, in the bowels of Christ, and concerning the truth of our hearts therein, have we appealed unto the Lord. ...And now we hear, that not only the deceived people, but some of the ministers are also fallen in this battle. This is the great hand of the Lord, and worthy of the consideration of all those who take into their hands the instruments of a foolish shepherd, to wit, meddling with worldly policies, and mixtures of earthly power, to set up that which they call the Kingdom of Christ, which is neither it, nor, if it were it, would such means be found effectual to that end; and neglect, or trust not to, the Word of God, the sword of the Spirit, which is alone powerful and able for the setting up of that Kingdom, and, when trusted to, will be found effectually able to that end, and will also do it" (Carlyle, *Oliver Cromwell's Letters and Speeches*, II, 216–217).

Elizabeth Cromwell

[From a drawing by W. Bond. Reproduced from Charles Firth, *Oliver Cromwell and the Rule of the Puritans in England* (London: G.P. Putnam's Sons, 1900)]

16

For my beloved Wife Elizabeth Cromwell [1]

Edinburgh, April 12, 1651

My Dearest,

I praise the Lord I am increased in strength in my outward man. But that will not satisfy me except I get a heart to love and serve my heavenly Father better; and get more of the light of his countenance, which is better than life,[2] and more power over my corruptions. In these hopes I wait, and am not without expectation of a gracious return. Pray for me; truly I do daily for thee and the dear family; and God Almighty bless you all with his spiritual blessings.

Mind poor Betty[3] of the Lord's great mercy. Oh, I desire her not only to seek the Lord in her necessity, but in deed and in truth to turn to the Lord, and to keep close to him, and to take heed of a departing heart, and of being cozened with worldly vanities and worldly company, which I doubt she is too subject to. I earnestly and frequently pray for her and for him. Truly they are dear to me, very dear; and I am in fear lest Satan should deceive them, knowing how weak our hearts are, and how subtle the Adversary is, and what way the deceitfulness of our hearts and the vain world make for his temptations. The Lord give them truth of heart to him. Let them seek him in truth, and they shall find him.

My love to the dear little ones; I pray for grace for them. I thank them for their letters; let me have them often....

If Dick Cromwell and his wife be with you, my dear love to them. I pray for them: they shall, God willing, hear from me. I love them very dearly. Truly I am not able as yet to write much. I am weary...[4]

[1] Carlyle, *Oliver Cromwell's Letters and Speeches*, II, 296–297.

[2] Psalm 63:3.

[3] This is Elizabeth Claypole. The "him" mentioned a few lines down is her husband, John. On Elizabeth, see pp.63–64.

[4] In a letter that Cromwell wrote to his wife on September 4, 1650, the day after the Battle of Dunbar, he told her: "I grow an old man, and feel infirmities of age marvellously stealing upon me. Would my corruptions did as fast decrease" (Carlyle, *Oliver Cromwell's Letters and Speeches*, II, 221).

17

For my beloved Wife Elizabeth Cromwell[1]

Edinburgh, May 3, 1651

My Dearest,

I could not satisfy myself to omit this post, although I have not much to write; yet indeed I love to write to my Dear, who is very much in my heart.[2] It joys me to hear thy soul prospereth: the Lord increase his favours to thee more and more. The great good thy soul can wish is, that the Lord lift upon thee the light of his countenance,[3] which is better than life.[4] The Lord bless all thy good counsel and example to all those about thee, and hear all thy prayers, and accept thee always.

[1] Carlyle, *Oliver Cromwell's Letters and Speeches*, II, 306.

[2] In a letter that Cromwell wrote to his wife on September 4, 1650, the day after the Battle of Dunbar, he told her: "Thou art dearer to me than any creature" (Carlyle, *Oliver Cromwell's Letters and Speeches*, II, 221).

[3] Numbers 6:26.

[4] Psalm 63:3.

18

For my esteemed Friend Mr. Cotton, Pastor to the Church at Boston in New England[1]

October 2, 1651

Worthy Sir, and my Christian Friend,

I received yours a few days sithence.[2] It was welcome to me because signed by you, whom I love and honour in the Lord; but more to see some of the same grounds of our actings stirring in you that are in us, to quiet us to our work, and support us therein; which hath had greatest difficulty in our engagement in Scotland; by reason we have had to do with some who were, I verily think, godly, but, through weakness and the subtlety of Satan, involved in interests against the Lord and his people.

With what tenderness we have proceeded with such, and that in sincerity, our papers (which I suppose you have seen) will in part manifest; and I give you some comfortable assurance of. The Lord hath marvellously appeared even against them....[3]

Surely, Sir, the Lord is greatly to be feared and to be praised! We need your prayers in this as much as ever. How shall we behave ourselves after such mercies? What is the Lord a-doing? What prophecies are now fulfilling? Who is a God like ours? To know his will, to do his will, are both of him.

I took this liberty from business, to salute you thus in a word. Truly I am ready to serve you and the rest of our brethren and the Churches with you. I am a poor weak creature, and not worthy the name of a worm; yet accepted to serve the Lord and his people. Indeed, my dear friend, between you and me, you know not me, my weaknesses, my inordinate passions, my unskilfulness and everyway unfitness to my work. Yet, yet the Lord, who will have mercy on whom he will,[4] does as you see! Pray for me. Salute all Christian friends though unknown.

[1] Carlyle, *Oliver Cromwell's Letters and Speeches*, III, 9–10. John Cotton (1584–1652) had been educated at Emmanuel College in Cambridge University. His piety and thought were strongly shaped by Richard Sibbes (1577–1635), under whose preaching Cotton had been converted in 1609. He was the minister of St. Botolph's Church in Boston, Lincolnshire, for over twenty years. During the persecution of Puritan leaders in the 1630s, Cotton sailed for New England in 1633, where he played a formative role in shaping New England Puritanism.

[2] An obsolete word that in this context has the meaning of "since."

[3] This would be a reference chiefly to the Battles of Preston (1648), Dunbar (1650) and Worcester (1651).

[4] Romans 9:18.

19

For the Right Honourable Lieutenant-General Fleetwood [1]

[1652]

Dear Charles,

...Salute your dear wife from me. Bid her beware of a bondage spirit. Fear is the natural issue of such a spirit; the antidote is, Love. The voice of fear is: If I had done this; if I had avoided that, how well it had been with me!—I know this hath been her vain reasoning.

Love argueth in this wise: What a Christ have I; what a Father in and through him! What a name hath my Father: Merciful, gracious, long-suffering, abundant in goodness and truth, forgiving iniquity, transgression and sin.[2] What a nature hath my Father: He is love—free in it, unchangeable, infinite. What a covenant between him and Christ, for all the seed, for every one, wherein he undertakes all, and the poor soul nothing. The new covenant is grace to or upon the soul, to which it is passive and receptive. I do away their sins; I'll write my law, etc.; I'll put it in their hearts; they shall never depart from me, etc.[3]

This commends the love of God: it's Christ dying for men without strength, for men whilst sinners, whilst enemies.[4] And shall we seek for the root of our comforts within us; what God hath done, what he is to us in Christ, is the root of our comfort. In this is stability; in us is weakness. Acts of obedience are not perfect, and therefore yield not perfect peace. Faith, as an act, yields it not, but as it carries us into him, who is our perfect rest and peace; in whom we are accounted of, and received by, the Father, even as Christ himself. This is our high calling. Rest we here, and here only.

Commend me to Harry Cromwell.[5] I pray for him, that he may thrive, and improve in the knowledge and love of Christ. Commend me to all the officers. My prayers indeed are daily for them. Wish them to beware of bitterness of spirit, and of all things uncomely for the gospel. The Lord give you abundance of wisdom, and faith and patience. Take heed also of your natural inclination to compliance.

Pray for me.

[1] Carlyle, *Oliver Cromwell's Letters and Speeches*, III, 29–30. Charles Fleetwood (*c.*1618–1692) had married Cromwell's daughter Bridget in June 1652, about six months after Bridget's first husband, Henry Ireton, had died. By the time that this letter was written, Fleetwood had been appointed the Commander-in-Chief of the parliamentary army in Ireland. The exact date of the letter is not known. Abbott suggests December 1652 (Abbott, *The Writings and Speeches of Oliver Cromwell*, II, 601).

[2] Exodus 34:6–7.

[3] Jeremiah 31:33; 32:40.
[4] Romans 5:8.
[5] Henry Cromwell (1628–1674) was Cromwell's youngest son. He served under his father's command in the second phase of the Civil War. In 1654 he was appointed Commander-in-Chief of the parliamentary army in Ireland. He became the Lord Deputy of Ireland in 1657. At the restoration of the monarchy, he was allowed to live unmolested in retirement.

20

Speech to the Barebones Parliament [1]

July 4, 1653

...I think I need not advise, much less press you, to endeavour the promoting of the Gospel, to encourage the ministry, such a ministry and such ministers as be faithful in the land, upon whom the true character is. Men that have truly received the Spirit for such a use, which Christians will be able to discern, ...men that have received gifts from him that ascended on high and led captivity captive, for the work before mentioned [i.e. the ministry].[2] And truly the Apostle, speaking in another place, in the twelfth [chapter] of the Romans, when he has summed up all the mercies of God, and the goodness of God, and discoursed of the foundations of the Gospel, and of those things that are the subject of those first eleven chapters, after he hath besought them to offer up their souls and bodies a living sacrifice to God, he beseecheth them not to esteem more highly of themselves than they ought, but that they would be humble and sober-minded, and not stretch themselves beyond their line, but they would have a care to those that had received gifts to these uses there mentioned.[3] I speak not—I thank God it is far from my heart—for a ministry deriving itself from the Papacy, and pretending to that which is so much insisted on, "succession." The true succession is through the Spirit, given in that measure that the Spirit is given; and that is a right succession. But I need not discourse of these things to you; I am persuaded you are taught of God, in a greater measure than myself, concerning these things.

...It ought to be the longing of our hearts to see men brought to own the interest of Jesus Christ. And give me leave to say that, if I know anything in the world, what is there more like to win the people to the interest of Jesus Christ, to the love of godliness (nay what stronger duty lies upon you, being thus called [to be members of Parliament]), but an humble and godly conversation? So that they may see you love them, [that] you lay out yourselves, time and spirits, for them! Is not this the likeliest way to bring them to their liberties? And do not you, by this, put it upon God to find out times and seasons for it by pouring forth his Spirit? At least by convincing them that, as men fearing God have fought them out of their thraldom and bondage under the regal power, so men fearing God do now rule them in the fear of God, and take care to administer good unto them.

[1] Carlyle, *Oliver Cromwell's Letters and Speeches*, III, 61–62, 64. The so-called Barebones Parliament sat from July to December 1653. It derived its name from one of its members, Praise-God Barebone (*c.*1596–1679), a leather-seller by trade, who became a lay pastor in mid-1640. He was active in national and municipal politics during the 1650s.
[2] Ephesians 4:8.
[3] Romans 12:1–8.

21

A Declaration... inviting the People of England and Wales, to a Day of Solemn Fasting and Humiliation [1]

London, March 20, 1653

Do we thankfully acknowledge our mercy in the liberty of worshipping God in holiness and righteousness without fear, being delivered out of the hands of our enemies?

Is brotherly love, and a healing spirit of that force and value amongst us that it ought?

Do we own one another more for the grace of God and for the spiritual regeneration, and for the image of Christ in each other, or for our agreement with each other in this or that form, or opinion?

Do we first search for the Kingdom of Christ within us, before we seek one without us? Or do we listen to them that say concerning the coming of Christ, Lo here, and lo there?[2]

Do we not more contend for saints having rule in the world, than over their own hearts?

Are there not too many amongst us that cry up the

Spirit, with a neglect of love, joy, peace, meekness, patience, goodness, temperance, long-suffering, forbearance, brotherly kindness, charity, which are the fruits of the Spirit? How do we carry our selves, not only to the Churches of God, and the saints, but towards them that are without?

Do not some of us affirm our selves to be the only true ministry, and true Churches of Christ, and only to have the ordinances in purity, excluding our brethren, though of equal gifts, and having as large a seal of their ministry, and desiring with as much fervor and zeal to enjoy the ordinances in their utmost purity?

Do we remember old Puritan, or rather primitive simplicity, self-denial, mercy to the poor, uprightness, and justice? Or are we not herein put to shame by those we easily call anti-Christian or carnal?

Hath one that we judge to be without, equal justice with one we will call a brother?

Do we contend for the faith once delivered unto the saints,[3] as the things of faith ought to be contended for, with love, patience, tenderness, zeal, by persuasion? Or rather imposingly, proudly, carnally, provokingly, sensually, thereby prejudicing the truth and, whilst we are calling aloud for the propagating of the Gospel, do we not put stumbling-blocks in the way of the same, and too much endanger to make good the slander of the world in charging profession with faction?

[1] Wilbur Cortez Abbott with Catherine D. Crane and Madeleine R. Gleason, *The Writings and Speeches of Oliver Cromwell* (Cambridge: Harvard University Press, 1945), III, 226. This text forms part of a call to the nation to spend Friday, March 24, 1653, as a day of fasting and prayer.

[2] Matthew 24:23.

[3] Jude v.3.

Charles Fleetwood

[Reproduced from C.H. Simpkinson, *Thomas Harrison: Regicide and Major-General* (London: J.M. Dent & Co., 1905)]

22

For the Right Honourable Lieutenant-General Fleetwood[1]

August 22, 1653

Dear Charles,

Although I do not so often as is desired by me acquaint you how it is with me, yet I doubt not of your prayers in my behalf, that, in all things, I may walk as becometh the Gospel.[2]

Truly I never more needed all helps from my Christian friends than now! Fain would I have my service accepted of the saints, if the Lord will, but it is not so. Being of different judgments, and [those] of each sort most seeking to propagate their own, that spirit of kindness that is to them all, is hardly accepted of any. I hope I can say it, my life has been a willing sacrifice, and I hope,—for them all. Yet it much falls out as when the two Hebrews were rebuked; you know upon whom they turned their displeasure.[3]

But the Lord is wise, and will, I trust, make manifest that I am no enemy. Oh, how easy is mercy to be abused. Persuade friends with you to be very sober. If the day of the Lord be so near as some say, how should our moderation appear.[4] If every one, instead of contending, would justify his form "of judgment" by love and meekness, Wisdom would be justified of her children.[5] But, alas, I am, in my temptation, ready to say, "Oh, would I had wings like a dove, then would I [fly away, and be at rest. ...I would hasten my escape from the windy storm and tempest],[6] but this, I fear, is my haste. I bless the Lord I have somewhat keeps me alive, some sparks of the light of his countenance, and some sincerity above man's judgment. Excuse me thus unbowelling[7] my soul to you; pray for me, and desire my friends to do so also. My love to thy dear wife, whom indeed I entirely love, both naturally, and upon the best account[8]; and my blessing, if it be worth anything, upon thy little babe.[9]

1 Carlyle, *Oliver Cromwell's Letters and Speeches*, III, 74–75.

2 Philippians 1:27.

3 This is a reference to the account in Exodus 2:11–14, where Moses seeks to mediate in a quarrel between two Hebrews, and he becomes the butt of their anger.

4 At this period of time, Cromwell was attempting to broaden his base of support. In Ireland this meant attracting support from civilian quarters. A number of Cromwellian military officers in Ireland who also happened to be Baptists were not entirely happy with this new policy. See pp.113–115.

5 Luke 7:35.

6 Psalm 55:6,8.

7 A word now obsolete, meaning in this context to "unbosom oneself."

8 i.e. in Christ.

9 The baby in question may be Cromwell Fleetwood, who was born around 1653.

23

Speech to Parliament [1]

September 12, 1654

Is not Liberty of Conscience in religion a fundamental? So long as there is liberty of conscience for the supreme magistrate to exercise his conscience in erecting what form of church-government he is satisfied he should set up, why should not he give it to others? Liberty of conscience is a natural right; and he that would have it ought to give it, having liberty to settle what he likes for the public.

Indeed, that hath been one of the vanities of our contests. Every sect saith, "Oh! Give me liberty." But give him it, and to his power he will not yield it to anybody else. Where is our ingenuity? Truly, that's a thing ought to be very reciprocal. The magistrate hath his supremacy, and he may settle religion according to his conscience. And I may say it to you, I can say it: All the money of this nation would not have tempted men to fight upon such an account as they have engaged, if they had not had hopes of liberty, better than they had from Episcopacy, or than would have been afforded them from a Scottish Presbytery, or an English either, if it had made such steps or been as sharp and rigid as it threatened when it was first set up.

This I say is a fundamental. It ought to be so; it is for us, and the generations to come. And if there be an absoluteness in the imposer, without fitting allowances and exceptions from the rule, we shall have our people driven into wildernesses, as they were when those poor and afflicted people, that forsook their estates and inheritances here, where they lived plentifully and comfortably, for the enjoyment of their liberty, and were necessitated to go into a vast howling wilderness in New England,[2] where they have for liberty sake stript themselves of all their comfort and the full enjoyment they had, embracing rather loss of friends and want, than to be so ensnared and in bondage.

[1] Carlyle, *Oliver Cromwell's Letters and Speeches*, III, 147–148.
[2] This is a reference to the savage persecution of the Puritans by William Laud (1573–1645), Archbishop of Canterbury, during the 1630s. Many of the Puritans quit England to find religious freedom in the new world. It is noteworthy that some of them returned to England during the 1640s to fight on the side of Parliament in the Civil War. Laud's ritualism—the promotion of things such as clerical vestments, kneeling, bowing, and the communion table as an altar—his emphasis on complete religious uniformity, and the suppression of the Puritans were major factors in provoking the Civil War.

24

Speech to Parliament [1]

January 22, 1655

Cromwell gave this speech at the dissolution of the First Protectorate Parliament. In this section of the speech Cromwell is taking to task those who would accuse him of craftily engineering the vast social and political changes that had swept through Britain during the previous twelve years or so. He is convinced that they are of God.

"It was," say some, "the cunning of the Lord Protector…it was the craft of such a man, and his plot that hath brought it about!"… Oh, what blasphemy is this! Because men that are without God in the world, and walk not with him, know not what it is to pray or believe, and to receive returns from God, and to be spoken unto by the Spirit of God—who speaks without a written Word sometimes, yet according to it![2] God hath spoken heretofore in divers manners. Let him speak as he pleaseth. Hath he not given us liberty, nay is it not our duty, to go to the law and the testimony?[3] And there we shall find that there have been impressions, in extraordinary cases, as well without the written Word as with it. And therefore there is no difference in the thing thus asserted from truths generally received—except we will exclude the Spirit; without whose concurrence all other teachings are ineffectual. He doth speak to the hearts and consciences of men; and leadeth them to his law and testimony, and there he speaks to them: and so gives them double teachings. According to that of Job, "God speaketh once, yea twice,"[4] and to that of David, "God hath spoken once, twice have I heard this."[5] These men that live upon...their masses and service-books, their dead and carnal worship, no marvel if they be strangers to God, and to the works of God, and to spiritual dispensations. And because they say and believe thus, must we do so too? We, in this land, have been otherwise instructed, even by the Word, and works, and Spirit of God.

[1] Carlyle, *Oliver Cromwell's Letters and Speeches*, III, 190–191.

[2] This is a noteworthy statement that is at once typically Puritan and typically Reformed. In Cromwell's view, all that the Spirit does in the world and in the lives of human beings is "according" to the Word. But that does not mean that he cannot act apart from the Word of God, and impress upon believers his mind and purposes by means of providential events and the like. But these impressions are always to be tested by the Word and, for them to be genuine, they must always be in harmony with the Word. At its heart, this statement is an assertion of the freedom of the Spirit. See the very helpful discussion of this matter by Christopher Bennett,

"The Puritans and the Direct Operations of the Holy Spirit" in *Building on a Sure Foundation* (London: The Westminster Conference, 1994), 108–122.

[3] See Isaiah 8:20.

[4] Job 33:14.

[5] Psalm 62:11.

Henry Cromwell

[From a drawing by W. Bond. Reproduced from Charles Firth, *Oliver Cromwell and the Rule of the Puritans in England* (London: G.P. Putnam's Sons, 1900)]

25

To the Lord Fleetwood[1]

London, June 22, 1655

Dear Charles,

I write not often: at once I desire thee to know I most dearly love thee, and indeed my heart is plain to thee as thy heart can well desire: let nothing shake thee in this. The wretched jealousies that are amongst us, and the spirit of calumny turns all into gall and wormwood. My heart is for the people of God: that the Lord knows, and I trust will in due time manifest; yet thence are my wounds, which though it grieves me, yet through the grace of God doth not discourage me totally. Many good men are repining at everything; though indeed very many good [are] well satisfied, and satisfying daily. The will of the Lord will bring forth good in due time.

...Dear Charles, my dear love to thee; to my dear Biddy,[2] who is a joy to my heart, for what I hear of the Lord in her. Bid her be cheerful, and rejoice in the Lord once and again: if she knows the covenant thoroughly, she cannot but do [so]. For that transaction is without her, sure and stedfast, between the Father and the Mediator in his blood; therefore, leaning upon the Son, or looking to him, thirsting after him, embracing him, we are his seed, and the covenant is sure to all the seed. The compact is for the seed: God is bound in faithfulness to Christ, and in him to us; the covenant is without us, a transaction between God and Christ. Look up to it. God engageth in it to pardon us, to write his law in our heart, to plant his fear [so] that we shall never depart from him. We, under all our sins and infirmities, can daily offer a perfect Christ; and thus we have peace and safety, and apprehension of love, from a Father in covenant, who cannot deny himself. And truly in this is all my salvation, and this helps me to bear my great burdens.

...The Lord bless you all. Pray for me, that the Lord will direct, and keep me his servant. I bless the Lord I am not my own; but my condition to flesh and blood is very hard. Pray for me; I do for you all. Commend me to all friends.

[1] Carlyle, *Oliver Cromwell's Letters and Speeches*, III, 212–214. Fleetwood had been appointed Lord Deputy of Ireland in August, 1654.

[2] This is Cromwell's pet-name for his daughter Bridget.

26

For my Son Harry Cromwell [1]

London, April 21, 1656

Harry,

I have received your letters, and have also seen some from you to others, and am sufficiently satisfied of your burden, and that if the Lord be not with you, to enable you to bear it, you are in a very sad condition.

I am glad to hear what I have heard of your carriage; study still to be innocent, and to answer every occasion, roll yourself upon God, which to do needs much grace. Cry to the Lord to give you a plain single heart. Take heed of being over-jealous, lest your apprehensions of others cause you to offend. Know that uprightness will preserve you; in this be confident against men.

I think the Anabaptists are to blame in not being pleased with you.[2] That's their fault. It will not reach you, whilst you with singleness of heart make the glory of the Lord your aim. Take heed of professing religion without the power;[3] that will teach you to love all who are after the similitude of Christ. Take care of making it a business to be too hard for the men who contest with you. ...I know they are weak, because they are so peremptory in judging others. I quarrel not with them but in their seeking to supplant others, which is done by some, first by branding them with antichristianism, and then taking away their maintenance.[4]

Be not troubled with the late business; we understand the men. ...Lastly, take heed of studying to lay for yourself the foundation of a great estate. It will be a snare to you; they will watch you; bad men will be confirmed in covetousness. The thing is an evil which God abhors. I pray you think of me in this.[5]

If the Lord did not sustain me, I were undone; but I live, and I shall live, to the good pleasure of his grace. I find mercy at need. The God of all grace keep you.

[1] Carlyle, *Oliver Cromwell's Letters and Speeches*, III, 245–246. Henry Cromwell, Cromwell's youngest son, had been appointed Commander-in-Chief of the parliamentary army in Ireland in July 1655. Although he was not given the title of Lord Deputy, he effectively replaced his brother-in-law, Charles Fleetwood, who returned to England in September that year. Fleetwood retained the title of Lord Deputy until November 1657, when Henry was given the title.

[2] As noted on p.104, n.4, a number of Baptist officers in the army were critical of Cromwell's policies in Ireland. They became even more disaffected when he was installed as Lord Protector in December 1653. They believed that such a title was applicable to God alone. See Fraser, *Cromwell: Our Chief of Men*, 455–456. For a more detailed discussion, see B.R. White, "Thomas Patient in England and Ireland," *Irish Baptist Historical Society Journal*, 2 (1969–1970), 38–43; Marilyn A.

Hartman, "'For Christ and the People': The Ideology of the Good Old Cause, 1653-1660" (Unpublished Ph.D. thesis, Indiana University, 1977), 83–91; Kevin Herlihy, "'The Faithful Remnant': Irish Baptists, 1650–1750" in his ed., *The Irish Dissenting Tradition 1650–1750* (Dublin/Portland, Oregon: Four Courts Press Ltd., 1995), 68–72.

[3] Compare 2 Timothy 3:5.

[4] It would appear that some of the troublesome Baptists with whom Henry Cromwell had to deal were calling into question the Christian integrity of ministers who did not entirely share their convictions. Then, on this basis, they sought to have them removed from their pastoral charges.

[5] Cromwell is warning his son to steer clear of using political power to advance his own personal interests. This admonition is rooted in the father's awareness of the temptation to use his position as Lord Protector for personal gain, self-aggrandizement and the advancement of his family's fortunes. In fact, a charge that was made a number of times against Cromwell during his years as Lord Protector was that he was nothing more than a self-seeking hypocrite. This explains in part his sensitivity to the issue.

Robert Blake

[Reproduced from Thomas Carlyle, *Oliver Cromwell's Letters and Speeches with Elucidations* (New York: Charles Scribner's Sons, 1897), II]

27

To Generals Blake and Montagu, at Sea [1]

London, April 28, 1656

My loving Friends,

You have, as I verily believe and am persuaded, a plentiful stock of prayers going for you daily, sent up by the soberest and most approved ministers and Christians in this nation; and, notwithstanding some discouragements, very much wrestling of faith for you; which are to us, and I trust will be to you, matter of great encouragement. But notwithstanding all this, it will be good for you and us to deliver up ourselves and all our affairs to the disposition of our All-wise Father; who, not only out of prerogative, but because of his wisdom, goodness and truth, ought to be resigned unto by his creatures, and most especially by those who are children of his begetting through the Spirit. We have been lately taught that it is not in man to direct his way.[2] Indeed all the dispensations of God, whether adverse or prosperous, do fully read that lesson. We can no more turn away the Evil, as we call it, than attain the Good. And therefore Solomon's counsel, of doing what we have to do with all our might,[3] [and] getting our hearts wholly submitted, if not to rejoicing, at least to contentation[4] with whatsoever shall be dispensed by him to whom alone the issues of all things do belong, is worthy to be received by us.

[1] Carlyle, *Oliver Cromwell's Letters and Speeches*, III, 247. This letter was written at a time when England was at war with Spain. Robert Blake (1598–1657) was a firm Puritan. As Admiral of the Cromwellian Navy, he played a significant role in making the English navy an extraordinarily powerful force. In his early years Edward Montagu (1625–1672) appeared to be a firm supporter of the more radical Puritans, namely, the Independents and the Baptists. By the 1650s this support was waning. After Cromwell's death in 1658 and the rapid collapse of Richard Cromwell's government, Montagu quickly switched his allegiance to the royalist cause. Thus it was he who brought Charles II back from the Continent to England on board his flagship, the *Naseby*, later renamed the *Royal Charles.*

[2] Compare Jeremiah 10:23. Cromwell is referring to the defeat suffered by an English military expedition on the Spanish island of Hispaniola in March 1655. Cromwell had hoped that the attack on Hispaniola would ultimately lead to the overthrow of the entire Spanish empire in Central and South America. Cromwell learned of the debacle that July. The defeat had a profound spiritual impact on him. After much prayer and reflection, Cromwell eventually came to the conviction that the defeat was a punishment for his and for the nation's sins. See the detailed discussion of this incident by Blair Worden, "Oliver Cromwell and the Sin of Achan" in Derek Beales and Geoffrey Best, eds., *History, Society and the Churches. Essays in Honour of Owen Chadwick* (Cambridge: Cambridge University Press, 1985), 125–145.

[3] Ecclesiastes 9:10.

[4] This word, now largely obsolete, has the meaning of "acceptance" in this context.

The House of Commons as in 1656

[Reproduced from the frontispiece of the *Diary of Thomas Burton, Esq.*, ed. John Towill Rutt (London: Henry Colburn, 1828), I]

28

Speech at the opening of Parliament [1]

September 17, 1656

...I did read a Psalm yesterday, which truly may not unbecome me both to tell you of, and you to observe. It is the eighty-fifth Psalm, that is very instructive and significant; and though I do but a little touch upon it, I desire your perusal at [your] pleasure. It begins,

> Lord, thou hast been favourable to thy land; thou hast brought back the captivity of Jacob. Thou hast forgiven the iniquity of thy people, thou hast covered all their sins. Thou hast taken away all thy wrath, thou hast turned thyself from the fierceness of thine anger. Turn us, O God of our salvation, and cause thine anger towards us to cease. Wilt thou be angry with us for ever? Wilt thou draw out thine anger to all generations? Wilt thou not revive us again that thy people may rejoice in thee?[2]

Then he calls upon God as "the God of his salvation,"[3] and then saith he,

> I will hear what the Lord will speak: for he will speak peace unto his people and to his saints: but let them not turn again to folly. Surely his salvation is nigh them that fear him, Oh, that glory may dwell in our land. Mercy and truth are met together: righteousness and peace have kissed each other. Truth shall spring out of the earth, and righteousness shall look down from heaven. Yea, the Lord shall give that which is good, and our land shall yield its increase. Righteousness shall go before him, and shall set us in the way of his steps.[4]

Truly I wish that this Psalm, as it is written in the book, might be better written in our hearts, that we may say as David, "Thou hast done this," and "Thou hast done that," "Thou hast pardoned our sins," "Thou hast taken away our iniquities." Whither can we go to a better God, for he hath done it? It is to him any nation may come in their extremity for the taking away of his wrath. How did he do it? By pardoning their sins and taking away their iniquities. If we can but cry unto him, he will turn and take away our sins. Then let us listen to him, and then consult and meet in Parliament, and ask him counsel, and hear what he saith, "for he will speak peace unto his people." If you be the people of God, and be for the people of God, he will speak peace, and we will not again return to folly, [as to] which [there] is a great deal of grudging in the nation, that we cannot have our horse-races, cock-fightings, and the like. I do not think these are unlawful, but to make them recreations, that they will not endure to be abridged of them, is folly. Till God hath brought us to this spirit, he will not bear with us. "Aye, but he bears with them in France; they are so and so." Have they the gospel as we have? They have seen the sun but a little; we have great lights. If God give you a spirit of reformation, you will preserve this nation from turning again to these fooleries. And what will the end be? Comfort and blessing. Then "mercy and truth shall meet together." Here is a great deal of truth among professors,[5] but very little mercy. They are ready to cut the throats of one another. But when we are brought unto the right way, we shall be merciful as well as orthodox, and we know who it is that saith, that if a man could "speak with the tongue of men and angels," and yet want that, "he is but sounding brass and a tinkling cymbal."[6]

Therefore I beseech you in the name of God, set your hearts to this, and if you give your hearts to it, then you will sing Luther's Psalm.[7] That is a rare Psalm for a Christian, and if he set his heart open and can approve it to God, we shall hear him say, "God is our refuge and strength, a very present help in trouble." If Pope, and Spaniard,[8] and Devil and all, set themselves against us, though they should compass us about like bees, as it is in the hundred and eighteenth Psalm, yet in the name of the Lord we should destroy them. And as it is in this Psalm of Luther's,

> ...we will not fear though the earth be removed, and though the mountains be carried into the

> middle of the sea, though the waters thereof roar and be troubled, though the mountains shake with the swelling thereof. There is a river, the streams whereof shall make glad the city of God. God is in the midst of her, she shall not be moved.[9]

Then he repeats, two or three times, "The Lord of Hosts is with us, the God of Jacob is our refuge."[10]

I have done. All I have to say is, to pray God that he may bless you with his presence, that he who hath your hearts and mine would show his presence in the midst of us.

[1] Carlyle, *Oliver Cromwell's Letters and Speeches*, III, 307–310. Cromwell's opening speech to the second Protectorate Parliament may have taken two or three hours to deliver. This extract comes at the very end of the speech.

[2] Psalm 85:1–6. This psalm seems to have been much on Cromwell's mind during the final two years of his life.

[3] Psalm 85:4,7.

[4] Psalm 85:8–13.

[5] i.e. those who profess faith in Christ.

[6] 1 Corinthians 13:1.

[7] A reference to Martin Luther's famous paraphrase of Psalm 46, "A Mighty Fortress Is Our God."

[8] Cromwell viewed the Spanish as England's main military enemy.

[9] Psalm 46:2–5a.

[10] Psalm 46:7,11.

29

Dying sayings [1]

Cromwell spoke much of "the Covenant," of which there "were two, but put into one, before the foundation of the world."

"It is holy and true, it is holy and true, it is holy and true. Who made it holy and true? Who kept it holy and true? The great Mediator of the Covenant."

"The Covenant is but one. Faith in the Covenant is my only support, yet if I believe not, he abides faithful."[2]

"Whatsoever sins thou hast, doest, or shalt commit, if you lay hold upon free Grace, you are safe, but if you put your self under a Covenant of works, you bring your self under the law, and so under the curse, then you are gone."

Again thinking of the Covenant: "Is there none that will come and praise God, whose mercies endure for ever."[3]

When his children and wife stood weeping around

him, he said: "Love not this world, I say unto you, it is not good that you should love the world. Children, live like Christians, and I leave you the Covenant to feed upon."

"Is there none that says, who will deliver me from the peril? Man can do nothing, but God can do what he will."

"Lord, thou knowest, if I do desire to live, it is to show forth thy praise and declare thy works."

Once he was heard saying, "It is a fearful thing to fall into the hands of the living God."[4] This was spoken three times with great vehemency of spirit.

"All the promises of God are in him; yes, and in him Amen; to the glory of God by us, by us in Jesus Christ."[5]

"The Lord hath filled me with as much assurance of his pardon, and his love, as my soul can hold."

"I think I am the poorest wretch that lives; but I love God, or rather, am beloved of God."

"I am a conqueror, and more than a conqueror, through Christ that strengtheneth me."[6]

"Truly God is good; indeed he is; he will not [leave me]."

"I would be willing to live to be farther serviceable

to God and his people; but my work is done. Yet God will be with his people."

[1] Carlyle, *Oliver Cromwell's Letters and Speeches*, IV, 202–203, 205.

[2] 2 Timothy 2:13.

[3] Psalm 136.

[4] Hebrews 10:31.

[5] 2 Corinthians 1:20.

[6] Romans 8:37; Philippians 4:13. It will be recalled that Philippians 4:13 was an important text for Cromwell. See p.52, n.3.

30

Prayer [1]

Lord, though I am a miserable and wretched creature, I am in covenant with thee through grace. And I may, I will, come to thee, for thy people. Thou hast made me, though very unworthy, a mean instrument to do them some good, and thee service; and many of them have set too high a value upon me, though others wish and would be glad of my death; Lord, however thou do dispose of me, continue and go on to do good for them. Give them consistency of judgment, one heart, and mutual love; and go on to deliver them, and with the work of reformation; and make the Name of Christ glorious in the world. Teach those who look too much on thy instruments, to depend more upon thyself. Pardon such as desire to trample upon the dust of a poor worm, for they are thy people too. And pardon the folly of this short prayer:—Even for Jesus Christ's sake. And give us a good night, if it be thy pleasure. Amen.

[1] Carlyle, *Oliver Cromwell's Letters and Speeches*, IV, 204–205. This prayer was taken down by a number of those who were present at Cromwell's deathbed.

Select bibliography

Buchan, John. *Oliver Cromwell.* London: Hodder and Stoughton, Ltd., 1934.

Cocks, H.F. Lovell. *The Religious Life of Oliver Cromwell.* London: Independent Press Ltd., 1960.

Coward, Barry. *Cromwell.* London: Longman, 1991.

Davis, J.C. "Cromwell's religion." In *Oliver Cromwell and the English Revolution*, edited by John Morrill, 181–208. London/New York: Longman Group Ltd., 1990.

Drake, George A. "Oliver Cromwell and the Quest for Religious Toleration." In *The Impact of the Church Upon Its Culture*, edited by Jerald C. Brauer, 267–291. Chicago: The University of Chicago Press, 1968.

Fraser, Antonia. *Cromwell. Our Chief of Men.* London: Weidenfeld and Nicolson, 1973.

Gaunt, Peter. *Oliver Cromwell.* Oxford/Malden, Massachusetts: Blackwell Publishers, 1996.

Hill, Christopher. *God's Englishman: Oliver Cromwell and the English Revolution.* New York: Harper & Row, 1972.

Howell, Roger Jr. "Cromwell and English Liberty." In *Freedom and the English Revolution. Essays in History and Literature*, edited by R.C. Richardson and G.M. Ridden, 25–44. Manchester: Manchester University Press, 1986.

New, John F.H. "Cromwell and the Paradoxes of Puritanism." In *The Journal of British Studies*, 5, No.1 (November 1965), 53–59.

Paul, Robert S. *The Lord Protector: Religion and Politics in the Life of Oliver Cromwell.* Grand Rapids: William B. Eerdmans, 1955.

Roots, Ivan ed. *Speeches of Oliver Cromwell.* London: J.M. Dent & Sons Ltd., 1989.

Worden, Blair. "Providence and Politics in Cromwellian England." In *Past & Present*, 109 (November 1985), 55–99.

Worden, Blair. "Oliver Cromwell and the Sin of Achan." In *History, Society and the Churches. Essays in Honour of Owen Chadwick*, edited by Derek Beales and Geoffrey Best, 125–145. Cambridge: Cambridge University Press, 1985.

Worden, Blair. "Toleration and the Cromwellian Protectorate." In *Persecution and Toleration*, edited by W.J. Sheils, 199–233. Oxford: Basil Blackwell for The Ecclesiastical History Society, 1984.

Reading spiritual classics

In recent days, "spirituality" has become something of a buzzword in society. People seem concerned about the deeper "soul" realities of life. This is encouraging to see but there is a downside as well. The spiritual books being read are quite often drawn from streams that are seriously deficient when it comes to the truths Reformed believers delight in. This series has been designed to partially fill this gap by providing choice selections from various Reformed writers.

The reading of spiritual classics should differ from other types of reading. One reads a newspaper, dictionary or textbook for factual information or immediate answers to questions but in spiritual reading one seeks to inflame the heart towards God as well as to inform the mind. Spiritual reading, as Eugene Peterson has noted, should therefore be "leisurely, repetitive, reflective reading"—it should not be hurried. Careful attention needs to be paid to what the Spirit of God is saying through the text and those readings which are rich in spiritual nourishment need to be re-read again and again.

Of course, when it comes to spiritual classics, the Bible occupies a unique and indispensable place—it is the fountainhead and source of the Christian faith. Anyone wishing to make progress as a disciple of Christ must be committed to regular reflection and meditation on the Scriptures. As David says in Psalm 1, a believer is truly blessed when he or she delights in the Word of God and meditates on it "day and night" (Psalm 1:1–2).

Christians, for many generations now, have found strength and nourishment by meditating on the Word of God. Often their wisdom and insight was recorded—either in books, diaries, letters, hymns or sermons—and some of these, having been preserved, we are in the habit of calling spiritual classics. Such classics have a way of sending their readers back to the Bible with deeper insight into the nature of the Christian faith and serve to cultivate a greater desire to seek after Christ's glory and his abiding presence in their lives.

—Michael A.G. Haykin